Geauga County: Ohio

A Pictorial History

By James J. Anderson
and Jeannette Grosvenor

James J. Anderson

Jeannette Grosvenor

This is book number 1757 of a limited edition.

This book is dedicated to Newton Bostwick Chapman by his wife, Norma, whose generous sponsorship paved the way for this book.

Mr. Chapman embodied much of what this history is about. That is, making the most of one's talents and resources, then serving the community. He was born in Chardon, January 3, 1909, and graduated from Chardon High School in 1926. After receiving his degrees from Stanford University in 1930 and Yale Law School in 1933, he served in the F.B.I. and then the U.S. Navy during World War II. Taking up his law practice in Geauga County, he served Chardon Village at various times as Treasurer, Councilman, Mayor, Village Solicitor, and a member of the Library Board. In addition, he served ten years in the Ohio State House of Representatives, representing Geauga County.

Mr. Chapman died on April 11, 1987, in Scottsdale, Arizona, but his final resting place is in the Mausoleum of Chardon Village Cemetery.

Design By Joan Croyder

THE DONNING COMPANY
PUBLISHERS
NORFOLK/VIRGINIA BEACH

Geauga County: Ohio

A Pictorial History

By James J. Anderson
and Jeannette Grosvenor

Title page:
Although Chardon has the greater reputation for snow accumulation, Burton certainly gets its share. The date is evident on the photo, and the location is the west side of Main Street looking north in Burton.
Courtesy of Carl Mowery

Copyright ©1989 by James J. Anderson and Jeannette Grosvenor

All rights reserved, including the right to reproduce this work in any form whatsoever without permission in writing from the publisher, except for brief passages in connection with a review. For information, write:

The Donning Company/Publishers
5659 Virginia Beach Boulevard
Norfolk, Virginia 23502

Edited by Elizabeth B. Bobbitt
Richard A. Horwege, Senior Editor
Designed by Joan Croyder

Library of Congress Cataloging in Publication Data:

Anderson, James J., 1947-
   Geauga County, Ohio: a pictorial history / by James J. Anderson and Jeannette Grosvenor.

     p.   c.m.
   Includes bibliographical references.
   ISBN 0-89865-790-3

   1. Geauga County (Ohio)—History—Pictorial works. 2. Geauga County (Ohio)—Description and travel—views.
I. Grosvenor. Jeannette, 1924-
II. Title.
F497.G2A53 1989
977.1'336—dc20
89-16990 CIP

Printed in the United States of America

Contents

Acknowledgments	7
Introduction	9
Chapter 1	
The Nature of Things	11
Chapter 2	
Here We Are	21
Chapter 3	
Blessed to be a Blessing	39
Chapter 4	
Reading, 'Riting, 'Rithmetic	59
Chapter 5	
In the Bulb There is a Flower	77
Chapter 6	
Nature is Sweet	97
Chapter 7	
Here to There	115
Chapter 8	
Getting Down to Business	127
Chapter 9	
Leisure — A Civilizer of Man	145
Chapter 10	
"...of the people, by the people,	
for the people..."	163
Chapter 11	
Loose Ends	177
Bibliography	183
Appendix 1	
Population Statistics	184
Appendix 2	
School Population by District	185
Appendix 3	
Geauga County Officials	185
Index	185
About the Authors	192

Thompson Silica Company was formed in the early 1940s, and purchased a large area of the ledge which is part of Thompson Township. The company invested much money in land and equipment to process the silica sand. Debts caused the company to sell out in 1947. R. W. Sidley Company, which already had a gravel operation in Thompson, bought the land and equipment, and in 1989 continues to process silica sand. Prior to silica operations the quarry operations removed blocks of stone from the ledges. These were very important in building stone bridges throughout Geauga County.

ACKNOWLEDGMENTS

The following people and organizations were especially helpful in providing history, photographs, and encouragement. Without such help, this book would not have been possible. We greatly appreciate the assistance of Julie Armstrong and Donna Lang of American Cancer Society, Anderson Allyn, Sr., Marian Bottger, William and Alice Bullick, Carl Mowery of Burton Drug Company, Jane Bushman, Nancy Calfee, Virginia Carlburg, Richard Childs, Jill Coder–Sestak of the *Geauga Times-Leader,* Cooperative Extension Service, Rodney Dillon, Jr., Raymond Dolezal, William French, Geauga County Historical Society, the *Geauga Times-Leader,* Kim Glenn, William Grant, Lloyd Herrington, Virginia Hyde, Dorothy Knapp, Lydia McNaughton, Leanne Pealer, Geauga County Public Library, Richard Roose of Roose Drug Store, Iola Schinagle, Garland Shetler, the Soil and Water Conservation District, Violet Warren, and Sylvia Wiggins.

INTRODUCTION

We welcome you, the reader, into a glimpse of Geauga County, Ohio. Glimpse is the appropriate term because time and space constraints have limited our ability to share everything we would like to share with you. As we dug deeper into the past and present of Geauga County, we found more and more interesting people and places. So, it's good that we stopped, or you probably would never have gotten your hands on this book.

We thought this to be a needed project. The last county history was published in 1953, and a couple of Geauga communities have produced their own histories since then. But much has gone on throughout the county, and it is our wish that these glimpses, from the settlement to the present, spark your interest to read more of the past. More importantly, though, we wish for you to look around you and see the heritage that is here and now. It is comprised of your family, neighbors, friends, workplace, church, school, and the community. We are extremely grateful to those people of Geauga County, who, throughout its history, have had the vision to share with us the heritage of their time, and the history given to them. We apologize to you who have shared with us, whose sharing we were unable to include in this book. Many hours were spent agonizing over what we could or couldn't include. We have tried to include as many people as possible in the photos and stories, for they are the most important part of this history.

We encourage you to record what goes on in your life, whether through photographs, audio tapes, video tapes, or writing. Journals and diaries have never lost their importance to mankind. If you are involved in an organization, whether business, service, or social, keep a scrapbook. Hold on to the history that you make, no matter how insignificant you may judge it to be in the present.

THE NATURE OF THINGS

The sun was trying to warm these fields north of Middlefield at the end of January 1982 but Old Man Winter was winning as the temperature was only twenty degrees and more snow was expected. Photograph by Doris Cook, courtesy of the Geauga Times Leader

Chapter 1

WILDLIFE

Undoubtedly, among the first impressions that drew early settlers to stay in Geauga County were the lush forests and the availability of fresh water. Although much clearing of trees had to take place for the planting of crops, it was obvious that plants grew well in the soil and received a balance of sun and rain during the growing seasons. It was not unlike the territory left behind in New England. The forests had an abundance of maple, beech, ash, oak, chestnut, basswood, cherry, whitewood, and black walnut trees. Found in those forests were many kinds of animals, some to be hunted for food and others to be feared. Early accounts of the settlers identify large populations of whitetail deer and some elk. With those large animals were large predators including bears, wolves, and wild cats. In fact the southern townships of Auburn and Bainbridge were said to have been infested with bears and wolves. Today, after many years of greatly reduced numbers of large animals, the deer population has grown back to the point where harvesting of the herd can take place on a limited basis, and there have been indications that some black bears have returned to the county. Smaller animals such as rabbits, raccoons, opossums, and squirrels are abundant. The population of their predators including weasels, fox, and coyotes seem to be growing. One reptile which early county residents encountered that present day residents are thankful for the scarcity of is the rattlesnake. The following is an account from the *Pioneer and General History of Geauga County* (1880 edition): "The early settlers of the town (Chester) found themselves surrounded by rattlesnakes, many of them four to six feet long. They had a hiding place on what is now Sand Hill in Munson. One morning, in spring, the inhabitants turned out on a war of extermination. They succeeded in killing about thirty, which thinned them out considerably, and relieved themselves of the annoyance."

In the 1980s, through the efforts of the Ohio Department of Wildlife and County Game Protector

Reno Reda, wild turkeys are being restocked, predatory birds are protected, and a greater balance of wildlife seems to be back in the area. The Geauga County Park District has also done a tremendous job of preserving natural areas in the county for flora, fauna, and wildlife.

A wide variety of song and garden birds can be found throughout the county. Game birds such as Canadian geese, and several varieties of ducks can be seen.

LAKES, RIVERS, AND STREAMS

Three major rivers pass through Geauga County. They are the Chagrin, Cuyahoga, and Grand rivers. The Chagrin and Cuyahoga have their headwaters in the county. Plum Bottom Creek, a tributary of the Chagrin River, feeds Lake Lucerne. Geauga Lake, which sits on the border of Portage and Geauga counties, was first named Giles Pond. Other lakes which greeted early settlers were Punderson and Aquilla (earlier known as Claridon Pond). In the 1920s the City of Akron in Summit County recognized its need to provide for the future water resources for the city, and began the Akron Watershed program. The city bought large amounts of land in Auburn, Troy, Huntsburg, Claridon, Burton, and Middlefield Townships, and by 1989 has created two large reservoirs, LaDue (Auburn and Troy) and East Branch (Claridon and Huntsburg). The lakes, rivers, and streams in Geauga County are home to such species of fish as bass, bluegill, crappie, walleye, Northern pike, perch, catfish, trout and scavenger fish (suckers, carp, chubs).

GEOGRAPHY

Geauga County is considered to be a rolling plateau. In general, it lies about five hundred feet above Lake Erie. Little Mountain, a cone-shaped sandstone butte, sits on the northwest corner of the county. Some of the unique land features in addition to Little Mountain include ledges in Thompson, caves in Russell, and silica quarries in Chardon and Thompson.

F. M. Leonard, Esq. writing in the 1880 edition of the *Pioneer and General History of Geauga County* describes Thompson and its ledges as follows: "In its geological formation the conglomerate or pebbly sandstone forms the underlying of the township. The well-known ledge at this place furnishes a fine exposure of the rock, and gives a rugged and very romantic character to the place, and many visitors are attracted to the place, especially during the summer season."

Ansel's Cave, actually several caves, was the subject and title of a book by local author Albert G. Riddle in 1893. The caves are now on private property near Russell Center, but at the time of the interurbans (1900 to 1925), they were a popular tourist attraction.

Oil and gas wells have appeared in the 1980s. Although an eyesore to most, they have tapped into a valuable resource for the county and its residents.

Several earthquakes have been recorded in the county with the most recent occurring in January 1986. The tremor, measuring 5 on the Richter Scale, lasted several seconds. The epicenter was in Thompson Township, and for those experiencing it, the seconds seemed like minutes.

WEATHER

One cannot talk about Geauga County without talking about the weather. By nature of its altitude and proximity to Lake Erie, the county is the heart of the "snow belt." In the winter, when arctic winds blow across the unfrozen lake, the freezing moisture is deposited on the first high ground available, namely Geauga County. Chardon and Thompson especially bear the brunt of these "lake effect" storms which don't occur once the lake freezes, usually by mid-January. One account in the *Pioneer and General History* of 1880 states that they saw snow in June and July of 1816.

Histories of the county chronicle many severe snowstorms and hard winters, but they also speak of times of drought. Having just experienced the summer drought of 1988, this would not surprise most county residents. The drought of 1845 was severe with no rain from April 1 until June 10 (little that day), then July 2 (enough to make the roads a little muddy), and no more until September. Fortu-

These rock formations at the Thompson Ledges Township Park have fascinated people since their discovery. One can see from these outcroppings how stone quarries became a practical utilization of natural resources.

nately, these are exceptions to the beautiful balance of summer weather that occurs in Geauga County.

Through the years several tornadoes have touched down in the county with extensive damage. The first recorded was on July 22, 1804. It destroyed nearly one-sixth of the timber in Chester Township, but, even more significantly, Dr. John Miner was killed by a falling tree. 1809 and 1812 charted a tornado each, both of them occurring in Chester Township. In April 1841, a tornado started on the hill west of Chagrin River in Mayfield and moved northeast through the northwest corner of Chester to Kirtland. Extensive damage was done to farms and trees along the path. On July 4, 1969 a savage twister touched down on Burton Square as well as other areas of the county. Many old, valuable maple trees on the square were lost, and much damage was done to homes in the area either by the wind or by falling trees. The damage was so bad throughout northern Ohio that the Ohio Bell Telephone Company needed help from Michigan Bell to repair the damage. One cable crew did most of the work in the Burton service area.

This outcropping of rock in the northeast area of Chardon Village was popularly called "Rocky Cellar." "Here for many years the town's young folk, family, and social groups gathered for picnics in the cool shade of primeval forest trees." (Pioneer and General History of Geauga County, 1953, page 263.) In the 1890s the "Rocky Cellar" was marred by the establishment of a stone quarry at the west end of the ravine.

Chardon has gained its reputation as "snow capital" with mountains of evidence through the years. This view of Main Street circa 1910 says "snow belt" without a doubt. The poles over the walkway normally carried awnings.

Patrick Lennon, age fourteen, and a friend, Craig Bowden, eleven, look at the damage done to the Lennon home on Sweetbriar Lane in Russell Township. A twister touched down in June 1980 in the County Line Road area, and headed eastward about an eighth to a quarter mile south of Fairmount Road.
Photograph by Deborah Naiman, courtesy of the Geauga Times Leader

Bill Morgan (left) and Jerry Hiscox, members of Burton Volunteer Fire Department, inspect the front lawn of Oscar Glasscock on Route 87 where a huge tree was knocked over by powerful winds that ripped through northeast Ohio on Monday, January 4, 1982. Burton's park was nearly devastated by the tornado of July 4, 1969.
Photograph by Neil Korey, courtesy of the Geauga Times Leader

The snow blower was called into play to make room for emergency vehicles after the storm of mid-January 1982. Chardon Street Department employee Rudy Breunig and co-worker Stan Dacklewicz worked during low traffic hours and at night to clear the drifted snow from roadways and from the parking areas around the park.
Photograph by Marilyn Whipkey, courtesy of the Geauga Times Leader

By January 29, 1982, Geauga had registered 84.4 inches of snow. Residents of the Park Avenue Apartments thought all of it had fallen in front of their apartments.
Photograph by Marilyn Whipkey, courtesy of the Geauga Times Leader

LaDue Reservoir is part of the city of Akron's (Summit County) watershed property which makes that city the largest Geauga County landowner. The reservoir was named for Wendell Richard LaDue (1894-1986), a professional engineer, who was the Superintendent of the City of Akron Bureau of Water Supply from 1919 to 1963. The six billion gallon reservoir serves as a recreational facility for boating, fishing, picnicking, camping, and hunting. Upland game, deer, and waterfowl hunting is permitted. Controlled duck hunting has been featured since the fall of 1965.

WHITLAM WOODS PARK
Pearl Road,
Hambden Twp.

BIG CREEK PARK
Robinson Road,
Chardon Twp.

WALTER C. BEST
WILDLIFE
PRESERVE
Ravenna Road,
Munson Twp.

SWINE CREEK
RESERVATION
Hayes Road,
Middlefield Twp.

RUSSELL PARK
Rapids Road, Troy Twp.

(216) 286-9504
285-2222 (ext. 542)
564-7131 (ext. 542)
834-1856 (ext. 542)

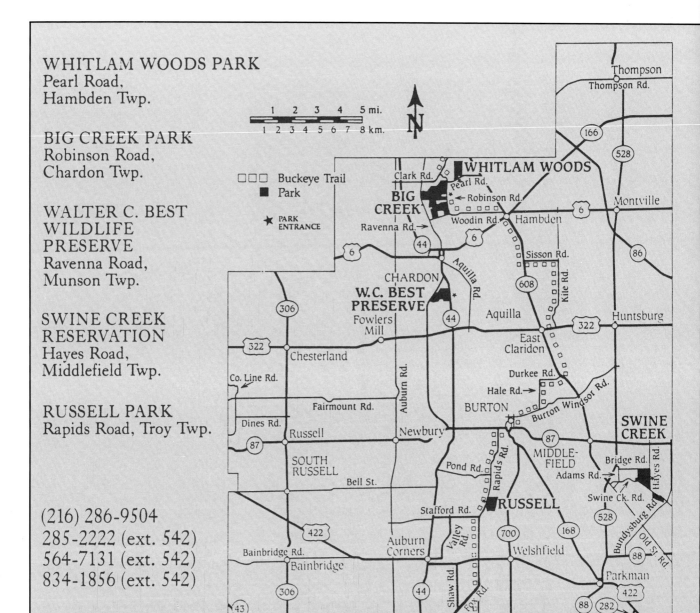

The Geauga Park District was established in August 1961 after initiation by the League of Women Voters and a hearing before Judge Robert Ford. The first Park Board was appointed in October of that year. Judge Ford appointed Mr. Kenneth McIntosh of Burton, Mrs. Upshur Evans of Russell, and Mr. Donald Linton of Munson. With the help of the Geauga County Commissioners, the four-acre Woodin Road Park opened in 1964. A tract of five hundred acres of land in Chardon Township north of Chardon had been left to the state of Ohio by the Mather family. Through the willingness of the State Department of Natural Resources and the passage of a county-wide levy in 1965 (second try), the Park District was able to lease what is now Big Creek Park from the state. Soon after the acquisition, Don Meyer was hired to supervise the development and construction of the park. The park opened in 1966. After years of volunteering, Duane Ferris of Burton became the first naturalist for the Park District. Russell Park (fifty acres) was dedicated in 1972. It was named for Eldon Russell of Troy in recognition of his years of service on the Park Board including president of the Board. Whitlam Woods was obtained in 1976, but point of access was only recently gained. Swine Creek Park was dedicated in 1981, and the W. C. Best Preserve was dedicated in 1988.

Spring pairs of Canadian geese await their goslings and summer visitors to the Lodge and Lodge Pond at Swine Creek Park in Middlefield Township. The Park is part of the Geauga Park District which is a real source of pride for Geauga County residents. In 1989 John R. O'Meara became Executive Director of the Park. The Park Commissioners in 1989 are Albert Lang, Mark Sperry, and Robert McCullough.

Phil Gingerich of the Geauga Park District tends Vicki and Charlie, the two Clydesdale horses who are the big hits with children of all ages at Swine Creek Park in Middlefield Township. Weekend wagon rides through the park guided by the rangers and volunteers provide an educational as well as recreational experience for park visitors. There is no charge for these tours, and the horses work from 1:00 to 5:00 p.m.

*On April 8, 1989, ground was broken at Big Creek Park for the Donald W. Meyer Center. Pictured are (left to right): Michael Butt, Don's grandson; Mary Lou Meyer, Don's widow; Jim Meyer, Don's son; and George Meyer, Don's father.
Courtesy the Geauga Park District*

*The Donald W. Meyer Center to be located near the Aspen Grove Picnic Area at Big Creek Park in Chardon Township is an appropriate tribute to the man who spent the last twenty-three years of his life making the Geauga Park District a joy and source of pride for all in the county. Don was the first park district director. Ground was broken for this building, designed by the architectural firm of Anthony Paskevich and Associates, on April 8, 1989, with completion expected in twelve to eighteen months from that date.
Courtesy of the Geauga Times Leader*

*Never mind the snow piled around the bottom of the time and temperature sign or the icicles hanging off the church, if you believe that signs don't lie. This picture of the Chardon Savings Bank (now Bank One) thermometer was published Monday, January 18, 1982. The headline in the paper, however, said that Chardon temperatures plummeted to minus nineteen degrees over the weekend.
Photograph by Marilyn Whipkey, courtesy of the Geauga Times Leader*

Much of the history of Geauga County has been making the most of what is there. Here is a scene that has become common throughout the still rural areas of the county. Oil and gas wells have proliferated in the 1980s taking advantage of the energy resources below the surface. At the same time, and often in the same fields, we find farm crops and animals utilizing the rich surface that abounds in the county. Not only have gas and oil finds been beneficial in easing the energy situation, but the income that the farmers derive and free gas available to the landowners have eased the burdens in off-crop or market years. Geauga County farmers have continued to prosper for the most part. One of the negative aspects of the process has been the dumping of brine used in the drilling process into nearby streams which has damaged some of the streams in the county. But closer enforcement of local, state, and federal environmental laws have nearly eliminated this problem.

HERE WE ARE

CHAPTER 2

Geauga County was created by the following legislative words on December 31, 1805, and was organized on the first Tuesday of the March following: "That all that part of the county of Trumbull lying north and east of a line, beginning on the east line of said county, on the line between townships number eight and nine, as known by the survey of said county, and running west on the same to the west line of range number five, thence south on said west line of range five to the northwest corner of township number five, to the middle of Cuyahoga River, where the course of the same is northerly, thence up the middle of said river to the intersection of the north line of said township number four; then west on the said north line of township number four to the west line of range fourteen, wherever the same shall run when the county west of the Cuyahoga River shall be surveyed into townships or tracts of five miles square each, and hence north to Lake Erie, shall be and the same is hereby set off and erected into a new county by the name of Geauga."

In 1810, all of that part of Geauga County lying west of the ninth range became Cuyahoga County. In 1840, seven of its northern townships went to the making of Lake County. Nine hundred acres from the southwest corner of Russell township—including a part of what is now Chagrin Falls—went to Cuyahoga County.

The sixteen townships of Geauga contain something less than four hundred square miles. The latitude of Geauga County is about 41.5 degrees north, and its longitude is about 81 degrees west from Greenwich.

"Five thousand pounds, New York currency, to be paid in goods to the western Indians, and two beef cattle and 100 gallons of whiskey to be paid to the eastern Indians, besides gifts and provisions for all of them." That, according to the old records, was the price paid by Moses Cleaveland, agent of the Connecticut Land Company, to "Red Jacket," principal chief of the "Six Nations," for the Indians' title to three million acres of land lying between the Pennsylvania line and the mouth of the Cuyahoga River on Lake Erie. The date was June 23, 1796.

The territory of this county belonged to the Erie Indians at the time of their destruction by the Six Nations. It was claimed by Spain, and it was a part of New France. Later it was England's and then it was a part of Connecticut, and then a part of the Northwest Territory.

Who was the first white man to pierce its forests and tread its soil? No one can ever know. A hunter from the East was in Middlefield as early as the middle of the eighteenth century.

The name, Geauga, is Indian, meaning "raccoon." It is a hilly county, there being a number of places rising about six hundred feet above the level of Lake Erie.

There were quite a number of Indians when the first settlers came. They are said to have been Tonawandas.

BURTON

The first permanent settlement within the limits of Geauga County was made in Burton in June 1798 (one record says 1796). Thomas and Lydia Umberfield and their five children arrived on June 21, 1798. By July 6, they occupied their new home.

There was an Indian camp along the Cuyahoga near the lower burial ground. Across the river on the sand knoll was a place for their dead. Likened to the Pilgrims of 1620, Burton's little population would have starved that first winter had it not been for the Indians.

Titus Street, one of the original owners, had a son called Burton. The town was named for the son and became a township in 1806.

In 1800 there were forty-two inhabitants in Burton. On July 4 they held the first celebration of Independence Day ever held in the county.

The first hotel was the Umberfield Coffee House. The Umberfield Log Cabin is part of the display of the Geauga County Historical Society. Visitors cannot imagine how a family of seven could live in so small an area.

Leroy Ladyzhensky of Lakewood and Nate Harvan of Garfield Heights were visiting the Apple Butter Festival in 1981 when they climbed on the wagon.

Can you imagine packing your family and all your worldly goods in a wagon similar to this and moving to Geauga County from somewhere in New England?

Emily Nash was six and one-half years old when the family of parents, five children, and a cousin moved from Plainfield, Massachusetts, to somewhere in New York State in the fall of 1812, In January 1813, they came on to Troy Township, arriving there the last of February. As the mother was driving the horse and wagon out of the yard in Plainfield, the horse spooked and ran the wheel up on a stone. The wagon was tipped over and all their "pork and beans" spilled on the ground.
Courtesy of Geauga Times Leader

Geauga County Historical Society officials and representatives of the Frohring Foundation, who contributed a sizeable donation for restoration of the Cook House, pose on the front porch at the dedication of the building in June 1980.

The group includes Mrs. Gertrude Frohring (seated second from left) of Newbury, along with foundation trustees Catherine and Wendell Felsgraf, and B. J. Shanower, president emeritus of the historical society. Standing (left to right): Mrs. Virginia Hyde, Maurice Fox, James Douglass, society president, and Bill Clapsaddle, who directed the renovation project.
Photograph by Doris Cook, courtesy of the Geauga Times Leader

MIDDLEFIELD

Middlefield was first settled in February, 1799 by Isaac Thompson and his son, James. They settled here after deciding that Mentor was too heavily timbered and the soil in Painesville was poor. On their way south to be closer to Pittsburgh, they stopped at the end of the first day and stayed for the rest of their lives. Joseph Johnson came from Pennsylvania in 1801. The township was first called Batavia and included Huntsburg. It kept the name until 1841, although Huntsburg became politically organized in 1821, but proved to have a double, to which the few letters were apt to go astray. It was called Middlefield having been, on the route just traveled, just halfway between Warren and Painesville.

The Cuyahoga River was a favorite resort for the Indians. Red Jacket is said to have visited the vicinity.

CHESTER

Chester was partially surveyed in 1796. Justice Miner was the first settler, coming in 1801. The town was early known as Wooster. It was named Chester for Chester, Massachusetts, because a number of the first settlers came from there. Although the township is Chester, the post office is Chesterland.

Sylvia Wiggins is somewhat a newcomer to Chester Township, but has collected and written its history in pictures and text. Sylvia was in on the inception of the Oral History Project sponsored by Kent State University, Geauga Campus. She interviewed hundreds of Geaugans on a variety of topics and transcribed the lion's share of the more than 450 tapes. Sylvia has indexed all of the material.

When the quarterly GEAUGANSPEAK was born in June 1975, Sylvia typed the stories under the direction of Dorothy Russell, the editor until September 1980. Violet Warren and Jeannette Grosvenor took over as co-editors in December 1980.

Geauga County and especially Chesterland are indebted to Sylvia for her efforts in documentation and preservation of its history.

The picture is labeled as "Isaac and Isabel Thompson, Founders of Middlefield." It is true that a Thompson named Isaac was the "Father of Middlefield," but he died in 1823. His wife's name was Jane, not Isabel. The pictured Isaac is probably a grandson. There is no record of his or Isabel's burial in Geauga County.
Courtesy of Shetler Printing/Roose Drug

"Bones of a prehistoric mastodon were unearthed recently in the township and are being preserved by the Cleveland Museum of Natural History... Nearly 20 bones were taken from a drained pond at an Amish residence in Middlefield Township last week. About five or six of the bones are in very good condition."
Michael Williams, curator of the museum's Vertebrate Paleontology department, said that the bones were from a sub-adult mastodon and are about nine thousand to ten thousand years old.

The huge mammal lived during the Pleistocene Period, grazing on shrubs in forests, rather than grasses like modern elephants. Mastodons were about fourteen feet tall at the shoulders, with tusks almost thirteen feet in length. The mastodon became extinct about eight thousand years ago.
Courtesy of the Geauga Times Leader, July 26, 1988, in an article by Denise Reynolds

Robert Green's property is about one-half mile north of Thompson and on the site of the quarry which was in full operation around the turn of the century. These are the marks of quarrying chisels.

Robert has made a showplace of the site in the rock gardens and plantings he has made. He made the basin for his Japanese garden.
Courtesy of Robert Green

The Chamberlin/Chamberlain family posed at their home in Hambden, probably in the late summer or fall of 1902.

Top row, standing, left to right: Ralph Chamberlin (1890–1963); Ethel Chamberlin (1888–1959) who married Ralph McNaughton; Amy and Anney Chamberlin (twins born 1883); Louise Chamberlin.

Middle row, seated, left to right: Elsie Chamberlin; A. B. C. Chamberlin (1860–1932); Inez Chamberlin (1898–1928) who married William P. Sturm; Rowena Belle (Strate) Chamberlin (1863–1937); Forest Chamberlin (1886–1956) who married Martha Winchell.

Front row, left to right: Roy Chamberlin; Marion (Dolly) ?, adopted 1903, Nelson (Pete) Chamberlin who probably hated being in a girl's dress; George Leo Chamberlin.

Alonzo Burton Chauncy Chamberlain, more familiarly known as A. B. C. was born in Woodhill, Steuben, New York, on March 2, 1860. He married Rowena Belle Strate in 1881. A. B. C., his brothers Orlando and William C., and their par-

Former Geaugan (Munson Township) Warren H. Miller of Bedford and Munson/Chardon Historian Maude Beech were interviewed at the June 1980 meeting of the Geauga Oral History Project. The interview was conducted by GOH secretary Sylvia Wiggins. It was about Munson store quarries and the activities of Miss Beech's father, George Washington Beech, who was a well-known stone mason in Geauga around the turn of the century.

Listening is Helen Coats of Burton who was interviewed for bulletin twenty-one (June 1980) of GEAUGANSPEAK. Thanks to Mrs. Coats, we have an artist's conception of the second courthouse built in Chardon in 1813.
Photograph by Doris Cook, courtesy of the Geauga Times Leader

ents Nelson H. and Dimas (Rowley) Chamberlin came to Hambden in June 1884.

Because of the shortage of doctors in the early days of Ohio settlement, A. B. C. became proficient in concocting a variety of home remedies to meet the needs of his large family. His "cure-all" advertisement appeared in December 9, 1891, issue of the Painesville Telegraph as follows: "Chamberlains Eye and Skin ointment, a certain cure for chronic sore eyes, tetter, salt rheum, scald head, old chronic sores, fever sores, eczema, itch, prairie scratch, Sore nipples & piles. It is cooling and soothing. Hundreds of cases have been cured by it after all other treatments have failed. 95 and 30 cent boxes for sale."

In 1907, A. B. C. moved his family to Texas. In Kingsville he continued his political interest and was elected as State Party Executive Committeeman from the Twenty-third Senatorial District. The family returned to Hambden in 1914.
Courtesy of Lydia McNaughton

THOMPSON

Dr. Isaac Palmer settled in Thompson in 1800. He came by boat from Buffalo to Fairport and up the Grand River. Palmer was not a permanent settler of Thompson because there was a disagreement with Mr. King, a landholder, on the division of the land. Palmer moved to Concord. The town was named in honor of Matthew Thompson of Suffield, Connecticut.

A journal was kept of the journey of the Bartlett family to Thompson in 1808. They left Southhampton, Massachusetts, on May 10, 1808, and reached Thompson, June 20, 1808.

The part of the township that is called South Thompson went by the name of "Burg" in the early days of its history. It was a prosperous spot and no less than seven waterwheels were operated on the stream nearby.

HAMBDEN
BONDSTOWN, OHIO

The township of Hambden was originally purchased November 8, 1798, by Oliver Phelps of Suffield, Connecticut. It contains 14,323 acres. Phelps sold 12,000 acres to Dr. Solomon Bond who came in the Spring of 1801 to look over his purchase. He only stayed here during the summer of 1801. Hambden was first called Bondstown, but the name was later changed to Hampden and then to Hambden. In 1810, the first cooperative society of Geauga was formed in the Bondstown Logging Society. This was a way to clear off property with the payment in whiskey. The organization only lasted about a year.

There was an encampment of Indians in the south part of the town in 1810. A squaw appeared at a doorstep with a naked papoose. The mistress of the house provided clothing for the papoose. The next morning, the squaw appeared a second time with the papoose again naked. This time the squaw was not successful.

PARKMAN

Robert B. Parkman was the first settler in 1804. The town was named for Samuel Parkman, Robert's uncle. Robert came with his wife, an infant son, and a brother-in-law, Alfred Phelps. The journey was made by land as far as Buffalo over roads so narrow that in many places it was difficult for the wagons to pass. It was so rough from logs and stumps that Mrs. Parkman often found it less fatiguing to walk and carry her infant child in her arms than to ride, while her husband and brother were frequently obliged to clear the road by the use of their axes.

The water power of the Grand River determined the location of the settlement. Parkman's first object was to secure the location of a road through Parkman. He was disappointed that it was so located as to pass only through the northeast corner of the township. This first road is known as the Mesopotamia Road and was laid out in 1805.

HON. ROBERT BRECK PARKMAN.
1804 Centennial 1904.

Robert B. Parkman died March 21, 1832, aged sixty years. Emily (Nash) Patchin wrote about his death as follows: "he was attacked by sickness when absent from home on business and died at the age of 61 after a long illness at Orwell Ashtabula County the memory of a good name which is rather to be chosen than great riches is the legacy which he left to his children and to the township to which he gave the strength of his early manhood and mature age he has laboured long to build good society in town."

Of Robert's wife, Lucy (Phelps), Emily says, "1820 August 9 the wife of Robert B. Parkman died to day at the age of 37 years after a long and distressing illness of consumption."
Courtesy of Alice Ferry; Shetler Printing/ Roose Drug

Parkman had its 175th anniversary in August 1979. The eighth generation of the Smith family was represented by Wade Warne of Middlefield and Douglas Smith of Parkman.

The first generation Smiths were Benjamin and Mercy who came in 1816. They died at the home of a son, at the ages respectively of ninety-three and eighty-six, in March 1831, with but a difference of a week in their deaths.
Courtesy of the Geauga Times Leader

The French family gathered at a Garrettsville home for this photograph. From left to right are: Avery Marvin French, born March 31, 1823, in Parkman; he is holding his granddaughter, Bessie French, daughter of Charles and Emma, born November 1, 1887; Charles Leroy French, born April 23, 1853, in Bundysburg; Emma Ella (Wolfe) French, wife of Charles, born February 21, 1860; Margaret (Day) French, wife of Avery; Lucy Northup; Hannah E. French, born February 18, 1852, in Otego, New York and the wife of Crosby who took the photograph. The young girl on the steps is Lorena Mae French, born February 24, 1881, in Garrettsville, Ohio; the boy on the steps (who probably hated the dress he was wearing) is Avery Marell French, born December 8, 1885, in Garrettsville.

Bundysburg is located in the northeast corner of Parkman and has a small cemetery. It is there that Elisha Bundy and William French, both soldiers of the Revolution, are buried. William French is the grandfather of Avery Marvin French. The 1880 history states that William died at the age of 104 years, but this does not check out with other records.
Courtesy of William French

HUNTSBURG

Huntsburg was first settled in 1808 but it had a "hermit" settler in 1802. John Finley supposedly was well-educated and came from Maryland. He was fearful of thunder and lightning and in such storms would run for the nearest settler. When the settlement "grew," Finley left in 1814. Stephen Pomeroy is claimed as the first permanent settler, but others could share "equal honors."

The town was named for Lewis Hunt who introduced improved fruit into the county. The survey of the township is unique in that the roads mark off the township in one-square-mile plots.

By 1812, there were six families with children in town and a small log schoolhouse was built at Barnes' Corners. There was no school tax in the very early days and those who sent children to school had to pay pro rata for the days the children attended school.

When Huntsburg published a souvenir booklet for their 175th anniversary, Hal Stanton contributed many anecdotes. One story he told concerned a Harpers Ferry musket.

"My grandfather, Luman Stanton, was known as a sort of male nurse ... In this case he had sat up through the night with Edgar Sober, who had inherited the musket. Luman had gone home to do his chores and eat breakfast. He was pretty blue as Edgar was one of his best friends. So he said to my grandfather, 'I'm afraid Edgar's time is about up. I must hurry back to be with him when he dies.'

"At this time she looked out of north window across the fields and exclaimed, 'He can't be dying for there he goes now with his old musket.'

"It developed that a red fox had ran through Edgar's dooryard and he had gotten out of bed, put on his clothes, loaded his musket and was tracking the fox in the snow."

A. G. Riddle was the prosecutor in the murder trial of Hiram Cole which was moved to Ashtabula County. Ranney, Sherman, and Thrasher made the defense. Riddle's reply to the arguments of Sherman and Ranney was said to be the most brilliant ever delivered in that region.

Emily (Nash) Patchin (of Troy Township) said, "March 1 1858 Mr Cole having his trial for murder in this county cruell man to murder a lovely woman to make room for a stranger women he did it to serve his master the devil".

Cole was acquitted, but the people condemned him, and he fled the country. Later (January 4, 1860), Emily wrote, "and I hear that Hiram Cole has committed another murder and is hung as he deserves without doubt by Judg Linch".
Courtesy of Marian Bottger

This is the way Huntsburg Center looked in the early 1900s according to a mural across the south wall of the Town Hall. Local artist Rev. Willard Strong painted it about 1965, and the picture was put in a souvenir booklet prepared for the 175th anniversary of the settlement of Huntsburg.
Courtesy of Violet Warren

Hal Stanton was a lifelong resident of Huntsburg and a descendant of one of the township's founding pioneers. He died in his home March 29, 1989, at the age of ninety-two.
Photograph by Doris Cook, courtesy of the Geauga Times Leader

NEWBURY

Lemuel Punderson was the first settler of Newbury, arriving in 1808. Judge Vene Stone claimed land in Newbury at an earlier date but actually lived in Burton. Newbury became a township in 1817. It was named either for Newbury, Vermont, Newbury, New Hampshire, or Newburyport, Massachusetts. During its early history, Newbury was divided into the north and south sections for business reasons.

Lake Punderson became the meeting place of the Pioneer Association which had annual meetings for many years at the turn of the twentieth century.

Proof that agriculture is a worthy pursuit is the fact that these men were all farmers (more or less engaged in dairying) who lived within one and one-eighth mile of each other in Troy Township and were all over eighty years of age when this was taken in December 1904.

Back row, left to right are: Levi P. Pool, born September 11, 1822, in Hawley, Massachusetts came to Troy in 1833; C. G. Corliss, born June 22, 1822, in Parkman, came to Troy in 1836; Harrison Hoard, born August 27, 1821, in Potter, New York, came to Troy in 1839; Dr. Laban Patch, born September 14, 1820, in Warren, New Hampshire, came to Troy in 1838.

Front row, left to right: Friend Dayton, born June 3, 1824, in Troy; B. H. Pratt, born July 17, 1824, in Troy; Thomas Kimpton, born August 16, 1824, in Ellsworth, England, came to Ohio in 1851 and to Troy in 1863; Henry L. Hosmer, born September 24, 1824, in Newbury, came to Troy in 1833.

Average age is 81 years, 8 months, 3 days; combined ages 653 years, 10 months, 5 days. Every one except Mr. Kimpton who is not a voter never having taken out naturalization paper, have voted for every Republican president who has received the nomination since the party was organized, and what is very remarkable six of the eight are total abstainers from the use of tobaccos and spirituous liquors.
Courtesy of Geauga County Historical Society

TROY

Troy was first settled by Jacob Welsh, of Boston, in 1811. He was accompanied by his daughter, Betsey. Jacob promised to give land to the township. When he reneged, a petition demanded a change. The center of town is called Welshfield, but the township is Troy. The name was probably picked because it was a favorite of one of the circulators of the petition.

Emily Nash came to Troy in 1813; she had her sixth birthday on October 28, 1812. She says at the beginning of a journal, "I will make me a little book to keep track of things along the way." It is obvious that the writing and sentence structure is not that of a child.

She married David Patchin and had a daughter Philansia. Emily suffered a severe stroke, which paralyzed her left side, before she was thirty years old. She blames it on "getting overdone at the raising of the meeting house." In spite of her debility, she outlived three husbands, her daughter and a grandson.

The journal details seventy-five years of life and change in one township of Geauga as Emily wrote faithfully until just before her death in 1888.

The journal is 441 pages long and has been transcribed using a word processing program called AppleWorks. Full names and dates were inserted and a second copy (fully indexed) was made. The original is in the possession of Charlene Whitney of Warren, Ohio. A photocopy and the indexed transcription are owned by Jeannette Grosvenor of Chardon, Ohio.

CLARIDON

The first settlers of Claridon arrived in Burton on August 6, 1811. Asa Cowles, his family, and relatives moved into a log tenement near the north boundary of Burton Township. From there they came to Claridon to erect their shelters. Claridon was first incorporated with Burton and was called Canton. In 1817 with McDonough (now Munson), the town was incorporated as Burlington. In 1819 a post office was established under the name of Claridon since there was another Burlington in Ohio. There is also another Claridon in Ohio. During the winter of 1819-1820 the name was changed to Claridon. The origin of the name is not known. One source says it was named "for a place in the east." There is a Clarendon, Vermont.

Lectrus J. Newell kept a small diary detailing a trip to Geneva, New York, to visit his uncle. "Oct. 20 (1857) Tues. Rode on the cars all night & at 4 found myself in Painesville and at 10 A.M. left for Chardon accompanied by many whose countenances were depicted with many a facetious smile. Was on the heights of Chardon at 2 PM. Staid at the convention a few minutes, then went to Claridon the land of steady habits."

In 1839, the county commissioners purchased the farm of Nathaniel Stone (on Aquilla Road south of Mayfield Road) to the used for a county home.

Even though the address and phone number of Geauga Hospital are both Chardon, the hospital is actually in Claridon Township.

A special word had to be coined for the 175th anniversary of the settlement of Claridon (then called Canton) Township in Aug 1811. The word was "Septuaquintucentennial."

The day dawned brightly; the Town Hall and Park were spruced to a fault. About the time of the program, the skies began to darken. Before long, a heavy rain dispersed the assemblage and spoiled the feastings.

History Professor Robert A. Wheeler, of Cleveland State University, researched Claridon through census, vital records, land records, clippings, and diaries. His paper was published in Ohio History. Volume 97, summer-autumn 1988, pages 101-121.

Sophia Taylor (daughter of Horace) was born in Claridon in 1815 and married Robert Rowley in 1836. The family assembled for this portrait about 1870.

Top row, left to right are: Fayette Rowley; Elosia (Andrews) Rowley, wife of Sherwood); Sherwood A. Rowley; Tracy D. Rowley (grandfather of Nancy Calfee); Addison H. Rowley.

Second row: Maria (Ensign) Rowley, wife of Fayette; Sophia (Taylor) Rowley, wife of Robert; Robert Rowley; Elizabeth (Williams) Rowley, wife of Addison.

Third row: Corydon T. Rowley; Celestia Sophia Rowley (adopted); Robert Rowley, son of Fayette; Ellen (Carter) Rowley, wife of Sherman; Sherman Rowley. (Sherman and Sherwood were twins born in Claridon in 1842).

Front row: Sophia Rowley, daughter of Fayette; Myra Rowley, daughter of Sherwood; Etta Rowley, daughter of Sherwood; Maud Rowley, daughter of Addison.

Tracing the parentage of Robert Rowley brought this to light: "Erastus Rowley gives notice that his wife Esther has left his board but not his bed since she took it with her and he will not be responsible for her debts." (From: The Painesville Telegraph, *1829*; abstracted by Judy Stebbins.

Courtesy of Nancy Calfee

BAINBRIDGE

Bainbridge was once called Austintown and Kentstown. It was named Bainbridge to honor a naval officer of the War of 1812. David McConoughey and his family (wife and six children) left Blandford, Massachusetts, November 9, 1810. The journey of nearly six hundred miles took fifty-three days. They stayed in Aurora and arrived on Thanksgiving Day in 1811.

The cabin was rudely constructed, eighteen by twenty feet, of round logs, with a huge fire-place, a puncheon floor made of logs split with the flat surface upwards, a stick chimney plastered inside with clay mortar, a cover of long split shingles held in place by heavy poles, one door opening north, and not a pane of glass in the apertures which served as windows.

The township was organized and named Bainbridge by the county commissioners, March 1, 1817. At that point, Auburn was included but was apparently set off by tax duplicate time in 1818.

Salmon (Solomon on his tombstone) Carver married Laura Clough on June 20, 1820, in Chardon. He was first married to Polly Brown by whom he had two children. He and Laura had 10 children. Their descendants are numerous in the area.

Laura's father, Amasa, was a soldier of the Revolution from Belchertown, Massachusetts. Amasa and his son, Jare, came to Geauga in 1813 or 1814. They were

Broken and neglected, these gravestones of Joseph Chamberlain and family were discovered on private property on Snyder Road in Bainbridge Township.

Chuck Warfield discovered several forgotten burial spots scattered around Geauga County. Warfield's hobby is hiking. His discoveries and copying of inscriptions were invaluable in publishing A Monumental Work; Inscriptions and Interments in Geauga County, Ohio, Through 1983."
Courtesy of Geauga Times Leader

Jonas H. and Lydia (Kingsley) Childs were early pioneers to Bainbridge Township. Jonas was born February 18, 1791, in Becket, Berkshire, Massachusetts, and was married to Lydia, also of Becket, in 1811. Jonas served in the War of 1812.

Jonas came to Ohio on foot in 1816 and bought land. In the winter of 1818, the Childs family came. There were now two sons, the oldest about three years old. The first task was construction of the log cabin. This was used several years when a brick house was built. Four more children were born in Bainbridge.

When the children were married and gone, the farm was sold in 1852.
Courtesy of Richard Childs

CHARDON

Chardon became the county seat in 1808, long before the first tree had been cut. Peter Chardon Brooks donated the land for the village plat to the county for the county seat on condition that the village be named Chardon. In 1812 Norman Canfield came over from Hambden and built a log house with a chamber. He was the first permanent settler of the township.

The fourth family to settle in Chardon was that of Anthony and Nancy Carter, who were black. In the winter of 1813, Mrs. Jabez King became a mother. All the ladies in Chardon were invited except Mrs. Carter. She was content to treat the matter with indifference, but her husband could not smother the insult and "black with rage" took his wife to Warren to live.

The only execution ever to take place in Geauga County occurred May 15, 1823, when Benjamin Wright was hung for the murder of Zophar Warner. The argument was over a debt of fifteen dollars. Emily Nash of Troy wrote an eye-witness account of the hanging. "as for me I felt that he deserved to be hung so I could see him struggle for life but it was an awful sight I hope never see the like again."

guests of Mr. and Mrs. Samuel King, who entertained them with all the cordiality consistent with their limited log cabin accommodations. At meal-times, the frugal housewife spread the economical repast upon a chest that had been brought from the east, and then was obliged to do double duty. Mr. and Mrs. King were short of chairs on this occasion, and, as a substitute, they used some pumpkins.
Courtesy of Jane Jevnikar

Lewis Gorman was born in 1795 in Connecticut. He came first to Painesville in 1818 and then to Claridon in 1820. He was a carpenter and was hired by Rev. Luther Humphrey to build a barn for which he was paid fifty acres of land. This land was located at Claridon Center, the south and east part of Lot 1, Section 12, south of Route 322 (Mayfield Road). Gorman is listed as the landowner in 1820 but not in 1830.

Hannah Rider was born in Massachusetts in 1804, the daughter of Benjamin Rider, the soldier of the Revolution who is buried in Rider Cemetery just north of the Chardon Middle School. Lewis and Hannah were married in 1825 and in 1850 were living in Chardon. By 1860 they lived in East Claridon where they both died, in 1868 and 1879 respectively.
Courtesy of Edith Lynn Mlaker

The Grant family members gather for a reunion and pose for this photograph during the summer of 1904 probably at the home of Leonard and Betsy (Marshall) Grant who are seated on the right. Grant Street (named for Leonard) which runs between South Hambden and North Hambden is the dividing line between Chardon Village and Hambden Township. The descendants of this couple are numerous in Geauga County and surrounding areas.

Top row, left to right are: John Grant holds his son Glen who was nicknamed Chicken; Grace Armena (Alderman) Hubbard Grant, wife of John called Minnie (formerly Mrs. Hubbard); William L. Grant holds his daughter Mabeletta (who became the wife of Otto Mumford); Noma A. (Trask) Grant, wife of William; Leonard Grant, Jr.; Carrie (Beach) Grant, wife of Orie; and Myrtle Grant is held by her father, Orie.

Middle row, left to right are: Arletta (Fox) Grant, wife of Charles Grant; Charles Grant; Leonard Grant, Sr., and Betsy (Marshall) Grant. Betsy was the daughter of Polly (Rider) Marshall and was born in Chardon in 1818. Leonard and Betsy were married in 1846.

Front row, left to right are: Edward Grant; Charles Grant (Dick); Lloyd W. Grant; Roy Robert Grant; Florence Hubbard; and Clarence Hubbard.

More information is available in the collection of the Geauga County Genealogical Society at the Chardon Library. Courtesy of William Grant

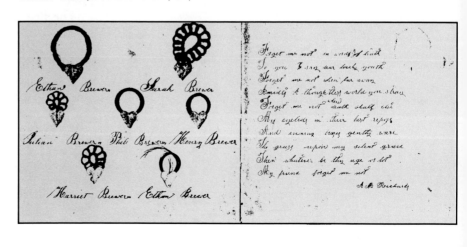

Austin and Sally (Chadwick) Richards came to Auburn in 1816. Their daughter was Almeda M. whose autograph book was filled with Auburn names and hair swatches which had been braided. Courtesy of Jean Fugman

Moses Barnes' application (May 12, 1833) for a pension for service in the Revolution was made while he lived in Montville. His record of his birth was lost in a fire when the house of Jehiel Willcox burned.
Courtesy of National Archives

William Brown was "warned out of Concord" as the town felt he would become a charge. He considered the notice a personal insult and said, "I cannot go tonight, sir, but I will tomorrow." Accordingly the family left the next morning and moved to Montville where he remained the rest of his life. He was quite celebrated as a Methodist preacher.
Courtesy of National Archives

AUBURN

Bildad Bradley first built a house in Newbury in 1814. When it was found to be on the wrong lot, he tore it down and moved it the following year to a site inside the Auburn line. Auburn is not a very hilly township and perhaps was named for that "Auburn, loveliest village of the plain," that the poet immortalizes.

Most township established villages at their approximate centers, which accounts for Auburn Center. But the older of the two, Auburn Corners, was founded partially because the first settlers located there and because two stagecoach lines intersected there.

MONTVILLE

Montville was surveyed in 1797. It is one of the most level in the county, though its name means "mountain town." It was supposed that much of the land is the highest in the county. Its first settlers came from Ashtabula County. They were Roswell Stevens, his son Reuel, and daughter Hepzibah. Montville was detached from Hambden and was settled into its own township in 1822.

On August 1, 1871, the bones of a mastodon were found on the farm of Royal Dimmick. Some of the dimensions reported were that the circumference at the knee was nineteen inches; hip-bones measured nearly four feet from one extreme point to the other; the largest of twenty ribs measured about five feet in length; and the tusk was nearly nine feet long.

MUNSON

McDonough was the first name given to Munson when it was included with Claridon. McDonough was a hero of the Battle of Lake Champlain. The name was changed to Munson after Monson, Massachusetts.

The first cheese factory in Ohio was the Maple Hill Factory established in Munson in 1862 by Anson Bartlett. Bartlett went to Rome, New York, to learn the factory method of making cheese. The second year he conducted the factory it worked the milk of one thousand cows.

The Munson Town Hall had to be prepared before it could be moved. Notice that the roof is ready to lift off, a necessity to clear the many wires it will encounter in its move to Burton, about nine miles away.

The stones that made the foundation did not make the move to Burton. They were hauled to the present township offices on Auburn Road and will be used in future landscaping projects.
Courtesy of the Geauga Times Leader

The Munson Town Hall takes a trip east of Mayfield Road on a Sunday morning in September 1987 to eventually become the Shanower Library at the Century Village in Burton.
Courtesy of the Geauga Times Leader

RUSSELL

Russell was the latest township to be settled because of the high price which the proprietors of the township set upon the land. The first settlers were Gideon Russell, his wife, and five children who came in 1818. They were the only inhabitants for nearly two years. When David Robinson (son of Clark) was six weeks old he started from Vermont for Ohio, in his mother's arms, on a pillow in a wagon. But few women would undertake a journey of five hundred miles under such circumstances. The Robinsons went first to Middlefield and then, in 1825, to Russell.

The burial of a soldier of the Revolution in Russell has not been proved, although there is a possibility in Jonathan Johnson. Gideon Russell fought in the Revolution. The township was named after him, but he is buried in Morton Cemetery in Newbury.

AQUILLA VILLAGE

With a little more than ninety-two acres and only two and one-half miles of roads, Aquilla Village is the smallest political subdivision in Geauga. In 1880, Judge Lester Taylor visualized an eagle's head in the outline of the lake. "Aquila" is the Latin word for eagle, but no explanation has been given as to why the double "l" in the village name. Before the change of name, the body of water was known as Goose Pond.

The village was first a summer colony. On September 20, 1923, the lot owners voted to incorporate.

See Appendix 1, Population Statistics

An application for a post office to be situated in the No. 1 track Lot No. 3 in Russell Township was submitted by Henry Hill "this second day of January, 1899." Along with the application was this diagram of the location.

Post offices have been known to botch deliveries, but a plus was the delivery of a letter to a resident in Novelty. The envelope simply said, "Unusual, Ohio." Courtesy of Sylvia Wiggins

*Gus Saikaly of the Geauga County Sanitary Engineer's Department explained the cost of a proposed sewer system for Aquilla Village. The residents met at Claridon Town Hall on August 29, 1981. The project was completed.
Photograph by Marilyn Whipkey, courtesy of Geauga Times Leader.*

BLESSED TO BE A BLESSING

A Wesleyan Methodist Church was organized in Russell. Briar Hill was built in 1851–1852. This view of the meeting house and cemetery was taken in 1910. The building has been restored and is now a museum.

The cemetery has two parts. Older residents call the old section Briar Hill Cemetery. The newer part is called Riverview. Across Fairmount Road (which is now paved but still narrow) is Riverview Memorial Park Cemetery.

Riverview Church is south on Chillicothe Road and is served by Rev. Robert E. Murphey.
Courtesy of Richard Childs

CHAPTER 3

THE WHITEWOOD BOARD

*Our fathers thought, in the years long past,
That a house or church should be built to last,
To laugh at weather, resist decay,
And still stand firm at the Judgement Day.
So they chose their wood with the utmost care
At a time when forests stretched everywhere,
And the writings left from that time record
That they made great use of the whitewood board.*

*For those trees grew tall, and their boughs spread
   wide
As they towered over the countryside.
It took them decades to reach their prime,
But before the white man they had the time.
So the builders sawed and they hewed and planed
Till the proper shapes were at last attained
And the structure was sided, roofed, and floored
With the help of God and the whitewood board.*
                            T. Dwight Ladd
                         November 21, 1977
                          (with permission)

The pioneers ranked religion and education near the top of the list of priorities in living in the "wilderness." Church membership was a sacred contract, and it was not taken lightly.

A candidate for membership in an early Congregational Church was expected to assent to the Covenant which included attendance at all institutions and ordinances of the gospel; a promise to promote the edification, purity, and peace of the church; and "endeavoring in all things to walk worthy of the vocation wherewith you are called."

A Standing Committee was charged with "the watch and care of members of the church." Excommunication resulted from "neglecting to commune with the church for more than a year past" and "unchristian walk."

In 1869, Mrs. Lavinia Goold asked for a letter of dismission from this church and of recommendation to the church in Orwell. "Voted that the request be granted and that the letter state that Sister Goold removed from among us twenty years ago or more."

Amish and "Yankee" life styles are quite different. Amish families have no telephones or electrical appliances. Their clothes are uniform and handmade. The women wear solid color dresses made in a distinctive style, black bonnets and shawls. The trousers that the men and boys wear are made with a flap in the front and are held up with suspenders. Their hats are broad brimmed and black. Beards are a sign of a married man.

The Amish do not accept Social Security, welfare, pensions, or other government handouts because they believe in taking care of themselves and their own. They do not believe in war, nor in bearing arms even for national defense. Members of the sect are accepted by the armed services as conscientious objectors. Many have served two years in hospitals as an alternative to military service.

Amish will not go to court to defend themselves nor will they file suit against another for whatever reason.

The Amish do not view the automobile as wicked but they will not own one. The elders believe it will trend toward breakdown of the family unit, and hence the basic structure of the community. They will ride in taxicabs, and many a "Yankee" makes a living transporting Amish to work in factories and homes.

The Amish insisted that the church should be an association of adult believers, which explains why their children are not baptized until they are about nineteen years of age. Each congregation decides independently its form of worship. They do not use churches, but worship in individual homes in weekly rotation.

Many of the Mennonites in the area were once Old Order Amish and have left that faith. Mennonites are more liberal in that they do own automobiles and have and use electrical appliances. Their dress is similar to the Amish, but more colorful. Mennonites and Amish do not have business dealings with each other.

By the time the 1953 history was written, it was evident that many of the churches had suffered some kind of division. Others had merged or disbanded, and new groups had moved in. With the advent of television, more single parent households, and working mothers, attendance dropped. Attendance during the last thirty-six years has also seen "mood swings" depending on the community or world situation, the pastor, the financial situation of the church and people, the Sunday School program, etc. Church organizations have a difficult time finding officers and volunteers.

World War II sparked a "We" philosophy. All groups worked together to preserve the freedom. When that effort was no longer needed, the "I, Me, Mine" attitude took over. Materialism, concern with physical appearance, "my rights," all have contributed to a self-centered attitude. As the decade of the '90s approaches, it seems that more people are realizing that there has to be something after the "here and now." May that realization make great strides.

A merger of Congregational churches and Evangelical and Reformed churches in 1963 resulted in the addition of UCC (United Church of Christ) to many church names. Seven UCC churches in Geauga County formed the Geauga Co-operative Ministry in May 1967. There are now nine members. Each church sends its pastor and elected representative to the monthly meetings. Among the activities are: Lenten Series, pulpit exchange, the Hausmann-Holmes Scholarship, sponsorship of a Vietnamese refugee family to live in Geauga, Men's and Ministers' Dinner, Junior Choir Festival, informational booth at the Great Geauga County Fair, and Youth Retreat.

Sesquicentennial Event No. 2 in the year-long celebration of the formation of the First Congregational Church of Claridon was a Home Worship service held at the home of T. Dwight and Elizabeth (Clark) Ladd on February 6, 1977.

The Rev. William H. Armstrong, pastor of the Burton Congregational Church, was supposed to ride up from Burton (about four miles away) to deliver the sermon. Since the temperature was four degrees below zero, Reverend Bill drove to Claridon Center where he was met by Kenneth Miller with a team of Welsh ponies. "Bud" Vaccariello is in the background recording the event.
Photographs by Doris Cook, courtesy of Geauga Times Leader

The Burton Congregational Church was organized in 1808. The building was built in 1834 and dedicated in 1836. In 1850, the building was moved to its present location. From a pamphlet prepared in 1984 by Jane Kay Gonczy, "The labor of moving the building was lessened by a generous application of soft soap to the planks along which it was rolled, and it has been suggested that this may explain why the affairs of the church have moved so smoothly ever since."

There have been major renovations in 1875, 1892, 1953, 1967, and 1983. It is interesting that the total cost of the original building was four thousand dollars and that the remodeling and annex done in 1953 cost seventy-five thousand dollars.

The Burton Congregational Church United Church of Christ belongs to the Geauga Co-operative Ministry. The Rev. William H. Armstrong is the pastor.
Courtesy of Geauga County Historical Society

The frame of the First Congregational Church of Claridon was raised in August or the fore part of September in 1831. The building was dedicated in September 1832.

This view has not changed very much since the photograph was taken about 1905. There has been some debate as to whether the church ever had a spire. The low building to the left of the entrance was the horse sheds. They were used other than Sunday morning by those who had automobiles and couldn't navigate the mud roads to their homes. The horses would be left there while the auto was used, and the shed served as a garage until the next trip.

The First Congregational Church of Claridon UCC graced the Standard Oil Company (Ohio) 1977 calendar. It was especially fitting because the church celebrated its 150th birthday that year.

The congregation had formed in 1827 and met, variously, in the home of Asa Cowles, the Kellogg schoolhouse, and the Center schoolhouse.

The Rev. Luther Humphrey reserved the "Handsome Whitewood" tree and gave it for use in building a meeting house in 1831. This tree stood just south of Mayfield Road on the west side of

Claridon-Troy Road and was ninety feet to the first branch. The circumference is not known. Legend has it that the wood from the tree provided the backs of all the pews in the church, the trim, and the wainscoting in the sanctuary.

The builders were Rufus Hurlburt and John Talbot who probably followed the drawings of Asher Benjamin, a well-known church builder in Connecticut. The building was dedicated in 1832 and was listed on the National Register of Historic Places in 1974.
Courtesy of Virginia Hyde

The Parkman Congregational Church was organized in 1823 with ten members as a Presbyterian church. The records of membership in the early years are very sketchy. In 1850, an attempt was made to build a church, but loss sustained by high water caused a long delay.

In 1873, there were only seven members. These seven made plans to build a church which they did and then dedicated the building on December 1, 1875. The only debt was one of five hundred dollars loaned by the Church Building Society.

The lot on which the church was sold in 1939. The church was moved up the hill by Andy C. Miller using one horse and a come-along type rig. It took one week to accomplish the move. At this time a basement was added. The rededication took place August 4, 1940.

The official name is Parkman Congregational United Church of Christ and it is served by the Rev. Lenn Zeller. The church is one of nine to make up the Geauga Co-operative Ministry.
Courtesy of Geauga County Historical Society

The Huntsburg Congregational Church stood on Church Street (now Easy Street), south of Mayfield Road (U.S. Route 322) and east of State Route 528. It was destroyed by fire during the morning of April 25, 1937, from an overheated furnace.

In 1836, a majority of the members declared themselves independent of the Grand River presbytery and organized as a Congregational church. The first building was erected at a cost of two thousand dollars. The church bell, at fifty cents a pound, was purchased in 1854 for four hundred dollars. In 1867, the building was moved west, across Church Street, and repaired at a cost of five thousand dollars.

After the fire, the church met for a time at a building on the southeast corner of Mayfield Road and Route 528. The Methodist Church occupied the building originally built by the Congregational Church south of Mayfield Road. The two groups worshipped together as a United Church. In 1959, at a cost of four thousand dollars, the Congregational Society bought out the Methodists, and the name became Huntsburg Congregational Church. (From Billye Sudyk)

Rev. Robert Barber introduces himself to the children at the children's sermon every Sunday as Reverend Bob. He usually brings a shopping bag with an object or objects related to the sermon. At the Junior Choir Festival in Burton on April 17, 1989, he used weights from barbells. The problem was that he needed help to take the weights to his car. One child doing everything would take a long time and would be hard work, but "Many hands make light work."
Courtesy of Violet Warren

In 1986–1987, the First Congregational Church of Claridon UCC was made accessible to the handicapped. The lay of the land necessitated a ramp for autos to discharge passengers at ground level and an elevator to give access to both the sanctuary and the Social Hall in the basement. The more than one hundred thousand dollar project also included relocation of the rest rooms, furnaces for natural gas, a new rear entrance, and redesigning the shed-type roof on the addition to the east end of the sanctuary. Until 1955, that addition housed the Sunday School and also was the location of the many church dinners.

The slogan for the Accessibility effort was, "Debt Free in Three." There were 216 active members at the time of the renovation, and the goal was accomplished.

The First United Methodist Church of East Claridon had its beginnings at Claridon Center. The building was constructed by Marcus Moffet in 1839 about where the present Town Hall stands.

Since the residents of West Claridon and Claridon Center were predominately Congregationalists, the Methodist Church struggled. In 1867 the building was drawn to East Claridon when a thorough repair was made and a steeple added.

The Rev. David West has a busy Sunday schedule. At 9:30 a.m. he leads worship services at Montville United Methodist Church At 10:35, the drive to East Claridon begins where at 11:00 a.m., worship at the First United Methodist Church of East Claridon begins.
Courtesy of Geauga County Historical Society

Montville United Methodist Church was built in 1836 by a community effort on a half acre of land purchased for twenty-five dollars. Rev. William Brown was the preacher, known by the familiar name of Billy Brown.

"His general custom, while preaching, was to stand behind a chair and fly, as it were, from one side of the house to the other, carrying the chair with him, stopping at short intervals, and bending low down over the chair, but never losing the thread of his argument. On one occasion, says an eyewitness, when leaning over his chair, he lost his balance, the chair tipping over, and he, turning an awkward somersault, striking on his feet, without causing any interruption in his discourse. The old ladies screamed, the young folks laughed, but he went on with the discourse, as though nothing had happened."
(1880 Pioneer History, page 769)

Montville Church of Christ is located just south of the Methodist Church. It has membership of all faiths. The pastor is Rev. David E. Detty.
Courtesy of Geauga County Historical Society

The Fowlers Mill Christian Church was built and dedicated in 1842. This building is now the auditorium of the present church. Rooms at the back were added in 1914. The steeple was erected in 1891, but there was no church bell until 1930.

In celebration of the 140th anniversary, a new entranceway, restored steeple, and landscaping were dedicated in September 1982.

The Rev. Roy Williams has two Sunday worship services, at 8:30 and 10:40 a.m. Adult Bible classes and Sunday School take place at 9:30 a.m.
Courtesy of Geauga County Historical Society

The Newbury Community Church was selected for the Standard Oil Company (Ohio) calendar for 1969 and 1985. The theme of the calendars has been "Let's Explore Ohio."

The church had its beginnings in 1845 when the Baptists and Universalists built a church at the Center. Within a few years, they moved to different localities. The Methodist Association rented the church for a time in the 1890s. For a number of years, no regular services were held.

Reorganization took place on December 5, 1943, and the name Newbury Community Church was adopted. The church belongs to the Geauga Cooperative Ministry. The Rev. Dana Welch was called to replace Pastors Edward and Shirley Malzer. Ed died of cancer while serving the church with his wife, Rev. Shirley Malzer. Courtesy of Marian Bottger

This is a picture of a painting of the South Newbury Chapel. When James A. Garfield was barred from speaking at the Congregational Church in 1856, the Union Chapel, dedicated to free speech, was born. The dedication sermon was preached by James A. Garfield.
Courtesy of Marian Bottger

The beginning of the Thompson United Methodist Church was in the fall of 1829. The first church was built in 1846, and this church was built on the same lot in 1884 at a cost of about six thousand dollars.

The Rev. Chester C. Rupert is the pastor. The Morning Star Coffeehouse welcomes all for music and fellowship from 7:30 to 10:30 p.m. Saturdays in the basement of the church.
Courtesy of Geauga Oral History

St. Patrick's Church in Thompson celebrated its first mass on Christmas Eve of 1959. Father Hugh Bode will complete fourteen years of service in March 1990.

The William Sidley family came in 1837 and were the only Catholics in Thompson until 1849. The first Catholic church was built in 1854 on Sidley Road. It was variously a mission from Jefferson and Chardon. In 1934, the church was enlarged in celebration of the eightieth anniversary of its founding. That building burned along with many of the St. Patrick's Cemetery records.

The Church on the Green at the Geauga County Historical Society was the First Disciple Church in Auburn. It was built in 1846. Eventually it became the Auburn Community Church. The building was offered to the Society. It was moved in October 1963 and opened in the fall of 1964. The basement is the site of many lunch/dinner meetings for various organizations. The meal is prepared by the staff and volunteers.

David and Philinda B. (Lawrence) Nutt came to Geauga County from Marty, Oneida County, New York in 1836 or 1837 and settled at Novelty in Russell Township. In 1853, they purchased a 163.86-acre farm there and built a house on the property probably the following year. The house is still standing at 14149 Caves Road.

The photographs were taken during the 1860s. David was born December 8, 1799, probably at Floyd, Oneida, New York and died February 4, 1872 in Russell. Philinda was born April 13, 1800, in Deerfield, Oneida, New York and died January 18, 1883, in Russell. They were the parents of sixteen children, fifteen of whom lived to adulthood.

David Nutt was one of the four men who purchased the property in 1850 upon which the Briar Hill Church and Cemetery were built. David and Philinda are buried in the Nutt family plot on the east side of the church. (From Rodney E. Dillon, Jr.)
Courtesy of Richard E. Childs

St. Helen's Catholic Church in Newbury Township celebrated its 25th anniversary in 1977.

The parking lot is full on the Bingo nights. At least part of the money raised is used to support the St. Helen's Unicycle Drill Team.

A Saturday mass is held at 5:00 p.m.; Sunday masses are at 7:30, 9:00, 10:30 and noon.

Courtesy of Geauga County Historical Society

The First United Methodist Church of Middlefield was originally the Methodist Episcopal. As a result of division in the ranks, there was a split, and two congregations formed, the Methodist and the Wesleyan Methodist. The Middlefield Wesleyan Methodist is billed as the oldest church in Middlefield. It is served by the Rev. Lawrence Burcaw.

The "other" Methodists prospered and found it necessary to build this edifice in 1908 and dedicate it in 1910.

The Women's Guild maintains a Thrift Shop. Contributions of discarded clothing are received from any willing donor. The clothes are offered for sale at greatly reduced prices. Any not sold after a reasonable length of time are given to a mission.

The minister is the Rev. Paul Whipple.

Courtesy of Shetler Printing/Roose Drug

This Baldwin electronic organ was donated to the Bainbridge Community Church through the efforts of Jean Cassel, organist at the church for over twenty years.

Cassel noticed an offer for a free organ in an area church newsletter and immediately called for details. Someone had donated a twenty-one thousand dollar organ to Ridge Road United Church of Christ, and the Baldwin was offered to Brooklyn United Church who did not have room for it.

The organ is solid oak and has a greater range (eight speakers) and a different sound than the old Hammond which was moved to the Social Hall. Photograph by Deborah Sekerak, courtesy of the Geauga Times Leader

The Philathea Class posed at the August Picnic of 1978 that was held at the home of Mae Burton in Huntsburg. Left to right are: Mae Burton, Mabel Johnson, Ava Town, Belva Yoder, Catherine Feltes, Doris Herrington, Hazel Ohl, Adelaide Owen, Hazel Ely, Mildred Askew, Lucie Town, Florence Popovic, and Pauline Cunningham.

Phileo (Love) and Aletheia (Truth).

This is how a group of young married women came up with the name Philathea for a Sunday School class of the Middlefield United Methodist Church. It formed in 1917 with Eugenia Thompson as the teacher. The class still meets on Sunday morning at church and also the third Wednesday of the month at someone's home. (From Lucie Town) Courtesy of Violet Warren

The Methodist Church at the north end of Main Street in Chardon was dedicated on June 27, 1886. The cost of the building was twelve thousand dollars. The lovely trees in front have long since disappeared to make room for wider sidewalks and streets.

When the new Methodist Church was built north of Chardon Square, this building was sold to the Chardon Assembly of God in April 1961. The Rev. Moolchan Mark Seenarine is the pastor. Courtesy of Geauga County Historical Society

This building was erected in 1868 by the Methodists. At the raising, a beam broke and injured several.

The church prospered for many years, but eventually the members died or moved away, and the church withdrew from the Methodist Conference. The church was open to all denominations and was called the United Protestant Church. By-laws were written in 1942 and a council selected to take care of business. The church is now called the Bainbridge Community United Church of Christ and is a part of the Geauga Co-operative Ministry. The present (1989) pastors are the Reverends Kim and Jefferson Wells.

When the Rev. Dr. Jack E. Belsom served the church, he composed several songs. "When the Spirit Says, 'Sing'" and "The Parting Song" were published in Songs from the Hills intended to enable fun and worship through singing in Outdoor Ministries. The date of publication is not given, but it was after 1983. Courtesy of Geauga County Historical Society

Julian Czar Teed was tolling this bell in the Chardon Methodist Church on 15 Nov 1859 when he was seized with a fit. He fell out of the belfry onto the roof, and then to the frozen ground, a total fall of fifty-five feet. Teed was only bruised and lacerated. He explained his fall as follows:

"I was tolling the bell for the death of Jim Fowler, one stroke for each year. He always said that if I ever dared to toll the bell for him, I'd have one of my bad spells and fall off the church; and sure enough, I swow, I did. I wouldn't do it again for two shillin's."

The bell was donated by Peter Chardon Brooks who promised to give a bell to the first church erected by any denomination in Chardon. This one weighed 686 pounds and cost $174.75. It has called worshippers since 1834 except for a period in 1905 when it was being repaired in Pittsburgh.

Rev. Aubrey E. Kirby examines it prior to its move in 1961 to the front of the new building just north of the village. A freestanding tower was built in front of the church, and the bell still calls worshipers. It was dedicated in 1989. (From Chardon United Methodist Church "In the Beginning," 1983, and Geauga Times Leader)
Courtesy of Chardon United Methodist Church

The cover of this booklet shows the three churches built by the Chardon Methodists. The building in the lower left corner was started in 1833 and dedicated in 1836. Zadock Benton, Jr., was on the building committee but did not live to see it dedicated. The building was moved west and is the first house on Center Street. The church in the lower right corner was begun in 1882 and was used by the Methodists until 1960. It is the last building at the north end of Main Street and currently serves the Chardon Assembly of God. The artist's drawing at the top shows the present church which was built in two stages, the educational center and sanctuary. The total cost of land, building, and furnishings for the educational center was estimated at $190,000, and the first service was held on May 27, 1960. The consecration services for the sanctuary were held on May 8, 1966. The estimated cost for that portion was $225,000.
Courtesy of Chardon United Methodist Church

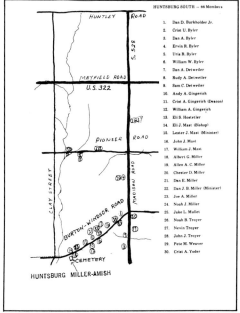

The beard is the sign of a married man. Mustaches do not exist in the Amish community. One man was married and immediately tried to grow a beard. Months and months went by before any evidence of facial hair appeared.

The black hat is for formal events; the working hat is not broad brimmed. It would be straw in the summer and felt in the winter.
Photograph by Perry Cragg, courtesy of Doris (Millard) Cragg

The Huntsburg South Amish church district is listed in the 1982 Amish directory as having sixty-six members. There are no church buildings as the members meet in the homes on a rotating basis. Districts are divided as the membership becomes too large for a home to accommodate.

There are forty-one districts in the directory. Twenty-eight of these have Geauga names. The number of members in a district varied from thirty-four members in Troy Northeast to one hundred seven members in Middlefield North. The head of a district is the Bishop. In addition, most districts have two ministers and one deacon.
Courtesy of Schlabach Printers

It is compulsory for women to wear coverings on their heads, indoors and outdoors. The black bonnet is for church, weddings, funerals, and shopping. The white bonnet is worn around home. It would be unusual for even a little girl not to have a bonnet. Perhaps she put it on her doll.

The most popular treat for Amish, young and old, male and female, is the ice cream cone. Stands selling frozen custard keep going on Amish trade. Photograph by Perry Cragg, courtesy of Doris (Millard) Cragg

It has been said that women build a church by their culinary skills. This is a different method of fund raising called a Service Auction. Members and friends donate a talent or service which is auctioned off to the highest bidder. Bill Richmond (on the tractor) offered one to five loads of manure delivered within a five mile radius of his home. Charles Poutasse donated his services for a nature walk. Alice Ozborne, auction registrar, recorded their donations.

Other items were: a will prepared by a competent lawyer, a Tempura dinner for five, a service call by a plumber with fifty years experience, a cake baked for a special occasion, and knitting lessons. Funds were being raised for a new roof.
Photograph by Doris Cook, courtesy of the Geauga Times Leader

The evergreen and the spire of the Chesterland Baptist Church are among the tallest structures in Chesterland. The main part of the church was built in 1870 at a cost of four thousand dollars. In 1944 the church was raised to put in a better basement. This was part of the 125th anniversary of the organization of the church.

The Rev. Dr. Kevin O'Connor serves as the present pastor.

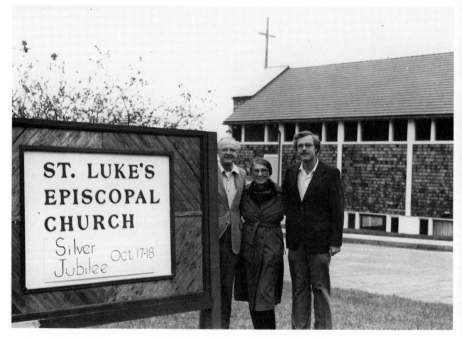

The co-chairmen for the Silver Jubilee (1981) of St. Luke's Episcopal Church on Wilson Mills Road in Chardon Township were Julia (Sheptak) Armstrong and Keith Tompkins (right). The pastor is Rev. Hugh Brownlee (left).

This church began as a result of an advertisement placed by Ed and Mary Hill in 1956 asking those persons interested in forming a local Episcopal Church to come to a meeting. About fifty persons attended the first service held on St. Luke's Day, October 18, 1956, in the Thrasher House on the Chardon Square. The building was erected in 1960 and is located at 11519 Wilson Mills Road. The Rev. William S. Brown is the Celebrant.

Photograph by Marilyn Whipkey, courtesy of the Geauga Times Leader

Elly Sabo, a member of St. Mark's Episcopal Church in Chester Township, donated a six-foot banner for Evangelism Sunday in January 1982. Rev. Richard Jesse is the admirer. He recently retired, and the church news in the Geauga Times Leader of May 1989 does not list a priest.
Photograph by Doris Cook, courtesy of the Geauga Times Leader

READING, 'RITING, 'RITHMETIC

58

CHAPTER 4

THE PIONEER SCHOOL HOUSE

We took a trip the other day
To a museum not so far away
We visited the one room school house there
And sat at an old fashioned desk and chair.
The thought of how they used the hickory stick
Was enough to make one feel quite sick,
There were McGuffey Readers and a slate board—
The Master's desk, water pail and gourd.

It was interesting to see—
How different their school house used to be.
I wonder if we would like to go
To school the way they did long ago?
                    A Fourth Grade Visitor

Besides field trips during the fall and spring, the building is used in the summer for Pioneer School; an idea introduced by Sandra Mueller who is the director. The school is a five day program of activities for those boys and girls ages nine through twelve or entering fourth through sixth grades. There is a morning session from 10:00 to 12:00 and an afternoon session from 1:00 to 3:00 at a cost of fifteen dollars per child. Each class is limited to twenty-five participants. The activities scheduled for 1989 were: a shooting demonstration; bullet making; sawmill demonstration; use of tools; dying cloth; stenciling; making ink, jam, ice cream, three legged milking stools, and taffy; wheat weaving; quilting; and square dancing.

The pioneers to Geauga County made every effort to see that "schoolin" was provided. Many times the same cabin that housed the church also served as a school.

The road to Amish education has not been smooth. The last recorded court case occurred in the 1920s when an effort was made to require high school attendance. Frank Schofield was hired as county superintendent and began a long career in January 1927. One of his first efforts was to reach an accord with the Amish bishops that the Amish would keep their children in school until they reached the age of sixteen, or through grade eight. The first "parochial" Amish school was in Parkman Township and opened for classes in 1950.

In 1968 a book center was built at the home of John Fisher, teacher of Newcomb Road School. This was done to handle the many schoolbooks which some public schools discard due to changing to newer editions.

There are two annual events at the Geauga-Trumbull schools, one is the spelldown for the eighth graders usually held in February. The German spelldown is held in the morning with the English in the afternoon. The achievement tests are held in April, again for eighth graders. This is their final school work.

While it used to be that each township was its own school district, the only one that retains the township boundaries is Newbury. This question was asked of the Geauga County Board of Education office, "How were these school boundary lines established?" No precise answer was available. If enough residents in a particular area petition the local school board and permission is granted, those residents go to that school district.

The County Board of Education used to set school calendars for the entire county. For about the last ten years, each school district has set its own. Berkshire contends with the dates of the Great Geauga County Fair; Chardon has to work around the Maple Festival. While Chardon is responsible for transportation to St. Mary's and Notre Dame, the calendars are different for the Catholic Schools. One advantage to this system however, is that graduation dates are different which allows grandparents to go to more than one grandchild's graduation.

For several reasons, not the least of which would be differences of opinion in public school philosophy, there is an increase in home teaching. This is arranged and supervised by the Geauga County Board of Education.

According to the *1985-1986 Annual Report of the Geauga County Board of Education,* 579 students received educational services through the SLD (Specific Learning Disabilities) programs. Along with that, every school district had a formal program for gifted students in the elementary grades, but no numbers were given. In the *1987-1988 Annual Report,* 350 students were served in SLD classrooms/learning centers and 150 in individual/small group instruction (tutoring). There was also a D.H. (Developmentally Handicapped) classification in 1987-1988 which served 156 pupils. The Gifted and Talented programs are not separate classrooms. The students are "pulled out" of their homeroom environment for a specified time each week. All of this is a vast improvement over the one-room/two-room school which had several grades and a full spectrum of physical and academic abilities.

In a survey of "Years of School Completed 25 Years and Over" from *The Lake County News-Herald,* Sunday, December 26, 1982, Geauga's percentage of high school graduates was 76.7. The highest figure was 91.4 percent for Russell, and the lowest was 47.1 percent for Middlefield. Russell's higher economic level and Middlefield's Amish population are reflected.

The battle of the tax dollar rages on. Every election has at least one school levy on the ballot. Ledgemont School in Thompson recently initiated a pay-if-you-play sports policy because a levy failed at the May 1989 election. Every school district has faced some crisis in funding. There has to be a better, fairer way than depending on the whim of voters and burdening property owners with most of the bill.
See Appendix 2, by District

Near the end of the 1979-1980 school year, Cardinal Middle School geography teacher Cindy Saydah rings the old schoolbell for the pupils to enter the Pioneer School. Some twenty-five girls, dressed in pioneer clothes, rode a schoolbus to Burton, made raffia wreaths out of cornstalks, did fancy writing with quill pens, and learned about many different skills required of the pioneer.

The schoolhouse on the Museum Grounds, looks today as it did when used almost a hundred years ago—the school bell, "flat top" stove, maps, water bucket, desks, hickory stick, etc. Children who visit the building, spell from one-hundred-year-old Spellers and read from McGuffy readers.
Photograph by Doris Cook, courtesy of the Geauga Times Leader

A first edition, mint condition McGuffey Fourth Reader: circa 1901, was given to Geauga County Historical Society director of guides and education program Gloria Armstrong and society trustee B. J. Shanower by George White of Middlefield. It had belonged to White's great-grandfather.

The presentation was made in front of the Pioneer School on the grounds on May 28, 1980.

Photograph by Deborah Naiman, courtesy of the Geauga Times Leader

While this map is dated 1981, it does not entirely agree with the map in the office of the Geauga County Board of Education. Cardinal includes pupils who actually live in Mesopotamia, Trumbull County.

Courtesy of Thomas Reap Realty

61

BERKSHIRE SCHOOL DISTRICT
(Burton, most of Claridon, Troy Townships)

Burton High School was the first of the large high schools built in Geauga. The general assembly authorized the school board to erect a $13,000 building which would "Be free to all youths of school age in the township."

With that money and a federal grant of $58,050, the new school was built on Main Street, just north of the stores. It was completed January 6, 1937. The major addition to the building front which includes the gymnasium and the cafeteria was completed in 1975. Through the consolidation of the Troy and Claridon school districts, it is now Berkshire High School.
Courtesy of Shetler Printing/Roose Drug

District (or neighborhood) schools were the pattern for education in Geauga County until the last forty years. In a one-room or two-room schoolhouse, the grades would be combined.

This was the entire population of Claridon Center School in 1929, grades one through eight. The school was a two-room building with grades one through four in the east room and grades five through eight in the west room. First row, left to right are: James Swonger, Harold Hausmann, Melvin Grover, Andrew Wellman, Stanley Malensek, Joseph Marek, Richard Starr, Charles Boehnlein, and Howard Litke. Second row, left to right are: Andrew Talarcek, Ernest Pollock, Dora Jean Webb, Mildred Webb, Matilda Hausmann, Ann Talarcek, Lottie Litke, June Grosvenor, and Jeannette Grosvenor. Third row, left to right are: Mabel Hossler, Teacher, Mildred Beech, Christine Malensek, Ursula Malensek, Milton Linden, Kenneth Wilmot, and Harold Kleinfeld. Fourth row, left to right are: Alice Marek, Mary Wellman, Elsie Talarcek, Linda Cook, Ann Wellman, Jean Wellman, and Loretta Hausmann. Back row, left to right are: Ralph Randles, Louis Malensek, Albert Babbish, Blanche Marek, Vivian Linden, Josephine

Talarcek, and Helen Babbish.

The same two-room building served grades one through twelve until 1912 when the last class (Ralph Grosvenor, Frank Kellogg, and Ralph Shanower) graduated from high school. Only the seventh and eighth grades used one room of the building during the school year of 1935–1936. After that all pupils went to East Claridon. High school pupils had a choice of Huntsburg, Burton, or Chardon. Tuition was paid, but transportation was up to the parents. The school stood vacant except for an occasional meeting until it burned about 1941.
Courtesy of June G. Kellogg

CARDINAL SCHOOL DISTRICT
(Huntsburg, Parkman, and Middlefield Townships)

The front entrance of Cardinal High School needs some identification. The rest of the building is left of the main entrance and toward Thompson Avenue where one finds the only sign. The new high school was completed in 1964, and has had three additions.

Thompson Avenue is one block east of the intersection of Routes 608 and 87 in Middlefield Village. The driveway is two blocks north of Route 87.

Julia Carr, Robert Aikens, Don Atwood, and Vince Dedek, Cardinal sixth graders, work on camp manuals at Cardinal's twenty-seventh year (1980) of School-in-the-Woods at Camp Burton on Butternut Road in Burton Township.

Nancy Speck, Geauga County Elementary Supervisor, does a Language Arts program which begins with "adopting a tree." After becoming acquainted with their trees, the pupils did a form of poetry called "line verse." An example selected from the Cardinal 1988 anthology is:

M assive
A ncient
P ure
L ovely
E xcellent

Photograph by Doris Cook, courtesy of the Geauga Times Leader

CHARDON SCHOOL DISTRICT
(Most of Chardon and Munson, Hambden, and part of Claridon Townships)

Chardon High School was built on East Park Street in Chardon Village in 1908. When the new high school was built, this building served various roles: the forerunner of the Kent State University, Geauga Campus; United Way offices; Chardon Board of Education offices; and mini-museum for the Chardon Preservation Society.

Elizabeth Carr, of the Chardon Historical Preservation Society, pleaded the case for rehabilitation of the 1908 high school in October 1984. The estimate for renovating the building was set at between five and seven hundred thousand dollars. Since no one came forward by the deadline of October 8, to present a financial plan, the buildings was razed over the weekend of October 8, 1984, much to the consternation of many Chardon residents.
Courtesy of Anderson Allyn

Do you remember hearing the stories of walking to school? "It was three miles one way." This horse-drawn "kid hack," the forerunner to the "big yellow bus," served Munson pupils.
Courtesy of Marian Bottger

Susan Vokoun of the Western Reserve Spinners and Weavers Guild demonstrated the art for Tina Marshall and Matt Kent during career week at Hambden Elementary School at the end of the 1979–1980 school year.

Resource persons in the area from dentists to police officers and artists spoke to students.
Photograph by Doris Cook, courtesy of the Geauga Times Leader

The Chardon High School at 151 Chardon Avenue was built in 1957 and has had several additions since then. High school students from Munson, Hambden, and the west part of Claridon go to this building.

The Middle School, the first in Geauga, opened in 1967 for grades six, seven, and eight.

When Mary Price retired from the Chardon School System in 1980 (after twenty years of teaching dramatics and related arts), it was estimated that she had touched the lives of over twenty-five hundred students. Here she honored some of them with a "break-a-leg" party at Park Auditorium.

There were two productions a year, a play and a musical: 1976–1977, Sound of Music and Romeo and Juliet 1977–1978 Guys and Dolls and My Three Angels; 1978–1979 Carousel and Arsenic and Old Lace; and 1979–1980 Fiddler on the Roof and Harvey.
Courtesy of Geauga Times Leader

Maple Elementary School pupils watched as a tree was planted. It was a living tribute to Esther Williams and Erma Mordoff who both retired from the school in 1980. The building is located on Maple Avenue in Chardon Village. Parent-Teacher Organization president Karen Titus assisted Esther Williams.
Photograph by Sharon Haynes, courtesy of the Geauga Times Leader

KENSTON SCHOOL DISTRICT
(Auburn and most of Bainbridge Townships)

Kenston High School was built in 1955. Its 1989 valuation is $6,700,000. The district combining Auburn and Bainbridge townships was formed in 1953 and named Kenston.

In 1966, the gymnasium was added. The Vocational Wing was constructed in 1973, and the Frank M. Tucek Science Center (also a wing) was built in 1986. In 1987, the cafeteria was extended, and the Board of Education offices were moved to the second floor above the cafeteria. (from Linda Hein, treasurer)

In 1980, Kenston High School's food services dining room formerly known as The Establishment was renamed The Betty Patton Room in honor of a former director of the school's vocational program. Mildred Lockert (founder of the restaurant) and Rita Kenny (vocational instructor) are holding the painting. Terry Talley made the plaque he is holding.

Mrs. Patton served the Kenston school system from 1961 until her death in 1978. She was instrumental in building the vocational program, particularly in the areas of home economics.

The Geauga County Retired Teachers Association had a luncheon meeting in The Betty Patton room in 1987. The menu, purchasing, cooking, serving, and cleaning up were responsibilities of the Food Service students. The room was also open to the public (on a regular schedule) for lunch.

Because of declining enrollment in Food Service classes, The Betty Patton Room closed in June 1989.
Courtesy of the Geauga Times Leader

Two members of the old Auburn Grade School, Mrs. Edna Burr (left) and Mrs. Cecelia Janson, president of the Auburn Alumni Association, look over the spot where the school building stood until it was torn down in 1952. The stone marks a special tree planting ceremony held in 1979 and was placed in May 1980.

Was it sent back to correct the spelling of Alumni?
Photograph by Doris Cook, courtesy of the Geauga Times Leader

LEDGEMONT LOCAL SCHOOL DISTRICT
(Montville and most of Thompson Townships)

This building was constructed as an elementary school in 1955, and became strictly a high school in 1982. The old Thompson High School on Route 528 north of the park stands idle and is deteriorating. The gymnasium looked huge in 1939 when arch rivals Thompson and Burton played a basketball game. The Loveland family dominated the Thompson team. The game was won when Kenny Janssen of Burton fired a shot from the center line and hit as the horn sounded.

Kindergarten pupils through eighth graders from Thompson and Montville go to the building on Burrows Road that was opened for the 1982–1983 school year. Montville Elementary School is used as a day care center.

A dress code was obviously in effect in 1919 when this group graduated from Thompson High School (now Ledgemont). Back row, left to right are: Wallace Green, Irma Andrews, and Homer Crandall. Middle row, left to right are: Maude Wilson, Margaruite Sullivan, and Walter Ernst. Front row, left to right are: Anna Wheeler and Janet Haldene.

Irma Andrews married James D. Sidley. She was a cook at the Huntsburg Elementary School for several years.
Courtesy of Jane Bushman

NEWBURY SCHOOL DISTRICT

Newbury School District is the only one in Geauga County where the school boundaries and township boundaries are the same. The building was the consolidation of eight one-room schools and the addition of a high school. The bond issue for $85,000 failed twice. An issue for $75,000 passed in November 1927. The building was built in 1928, and 124 students in 12 grades moved in January 1929. With addition to the building, over 900 students were accommodated in the 1988-89 school year.

In a festive mood for their annual homecoming celebration in the fall of 1988 are members of the senior class of Newbury High School, Class of 1989.
Courtesy of Newbury High School

WEST GEAUGA SCHOOL DISTRICT
(Chester, part of Munson, and most of Russell Townships)

The West Geauga High School was built in 1953. The gymnasium and shop area were added in 1958. Other additions in 1961, 1963, 1965, and a major addition in 1968 brought the building to its present capacity which reflects the tremendous growth that the Chesterland community has experienced.

Pupils in the village of South Russell and those living in a notch into Bainbridge Township go to Chagrin Falls (Cuyahoga County) to school.

The school that replaced the Geauga Seminary was opened in 1926 and closed its doors in June 1983. Since then, there has been much discussion as to what to do with the building. It served as a youth center for a brief time, but there was a problem with heating the facility. The latest problem is asbestos removal. Apparently it has to be removed for the building to be torn down. The cost to remove it in view of renovation is prohibitive.

PRIVATE AND PAROCHIAL SCHOOL SYSTEMS
AMISH SCHOOLS
(Schools are individual and under jurisdiction of the church district.)

Geauga County is dotted with Amish schools, and this building located at 15615 Durkee Road, Middlefield, is a typical example. The Ohio Amish Directory, Geauga County and Vicinity was published in 1982. There are twenty-five Geauga schools listed.
Courtesy of Shetler Printing/Roose Drug

GEAUGA CHRISTIAN SCHOOL
(Assembly of God)

Geauga Christian School students, Joel Smith, Wendy Kristoff, Dan Smith, Chad Mullett, and Shannon Redford looked over pledge lists for a Rockathon as they finalized plans for the mission benefit fundraiser of May 1980.

The Burton youth pledged a thousand dollars for the missionary equipment project.

Photograph by Doris Cook, courtesy of Geauga Times Leader

HAWKEN UPPER SCHOOL

The Walter White house is the residence of Fred Hoffman, Head of the Hawken Upper School, and his family. White was the president of White Motor Company. The twenty-three-room mansion was under construction when Walter was a bachelor, but in 1919 he married Mary Virginia Saunders. White was killed in an automobile accident in 1929, and Mrs. White lived until 1959.

Hawken was founded in 1915 by James A. Hawken as a boy's preparatory school through grade eight on Ansel Road in Cleveland. In 1960 the Upper School of Hawken (nine through twelve) was established on the White Estate in Gates Mills (Geauga County). In 1973 the Board of Trustees determined Hawken would become coeducational and by 1981, all thirteen grades were coed.

BESSIE BENNER METZENBAUM CENTER
(Geauga County Board of Mental Retardation & Developmental Disabilities)

Metzenbaum Center opened its doors in May 1965. The first full school year began on September 7, 1966, with fifty-nine children enrolled and four state approved classes; a pre-school class, and a Sheltered Workshop.

The Opportunity School started in April 1951 in the Odd Fellow's Hall in Burton for a six week trial with ten children. It moved to St. Helen's Church in Newbury, back to the library in Burton, and to the American Legion Hall in Newbury. Parents paid $4.00 per week tuition during those years. In August 1962, The County Welfare Department received approval to use county funds. The Bessie Benner Metzenbaum Foundation gave a grant of $212,000 and slightly more than twelve acres of land. The grant was contingent on passing an operating levy which voters approved in November 1964. The school also received federal funds of $22,000.

The new Metzenbaum Sheltered Industries became a reality in 1971. This facility provides employment for those beyond school age. The MSI Print Shop does everything from buttons to engraved signs. Most of the fifty-six issues of GEAUGAN-SPEAK, the Kent State University (Geauga Campus) Oral History Project quarterly were printed, stapled, and folded ready to mail in the MSI Print Shop. There are four residence halls. House A numbers a visually handicapped man and a seventy-three year old man among its residents.

Thursdays are lunch preparation days for students of Metzenbaum School in Chester Township. Working on items for the salad bar are Edna Miller (left), Kevin King (center), and Frank Learn. Teachers at the center buy the salads to provide students with some spending money. Photograph by Neil Korey, courtesy of the Geauga Times Leader

NOTRE DAME CATHEDRAL LATIN HIGH SCHOOL

Notre Dame Academy in Munson Township dedicated a new west wing which included ten new classrooms, a faculty study and workroom, a library-resource center, a student council office, and a bus waiting area. Construction took a year and a half and was dedicated by Bishop Anthony M. Pilla in May 1980.

Beginning with the school year of 1988–1989, the school became co-educational. The school was a merger of Cathedral Latin and Notre Dame Academy; its official name is Notre Dame Cathedral Latin. The freshman class had one hundred twenty girls and ninety-six boys.

On the same property, but almost a mile west, is the Notre Dame Elementary School.
Courtesy of Geauga Times Leader

ST. ANSELM SCHOOL

St. Anselm's is an elementary school. St. Anselm's Church had its seventeenth wine and cheese festival on Memorial Day weekend in 1989. It was estimated that seven thousand came through the gates.

ST. HELEN'S CATHOLIC SCHOOL

St. Helen's Catholic Church (in Newbury) unicyclists won four trophies by the end of April 1983, including two from the St. Patrick's Day parades. Showing off the trophies are from left to right: Wendy Gorris, age thirteen; Michael Reker, nine; Lisa Purdy, ten; Becky Haas, thirteen; and Advisor Carol Evans.

As part of physical fitness training, Father James J. Moran required students to learn to ride the unicycle. In an article in GO, The Goodyear Tire Dealer magazine, July 1969, it was stated that the program began "several years ago." Father Moran agreed to a proposal by Goodyear that the school's unicycle program serve as a "ride and wear" test for "Crazy Wheels," the company's new red, blue, green, orange, and yellow bicycle tires. In 1969 the school had a fleet of sixty cycles.

Most drills, stunts, and games are performed on standard three-foot-high unicycles, but some are performed on custom-built models ranging from five to eleven feet tall.

While it is no longer a requirement, the interest is keen and the St. Helen's Unicycle Drill Team performs in parades and festivals—some at considerable distance from Newbury.
Courtesy of Geauga Times Leader

ST. MARY'S CHURCH SCHOOL

St. Mary's Church School was built in 1960-1961 and was opened in September 1961 for grades one through four with 177 pupils. In 1965, eight classrooms were added so that the enrollment now is grades one through eight.

The first Catholics came to Chardon in 1859 and were visited by a priest twice a year. A parish was established in July 1909, and a small white church was built on the corner of Park and Ferris (across from the Chardon Village Cemetery). The church was moved to the east side of North Street, north of Chardon Avenue, in 1932. The priest lives in the house next door of the church.

The school does not have a gymnasium, and the children cross North Street for indoor physical education in the former sanctuary.

GEAUGA CAMPUS, KENT STATE UNIVERSITY

When the Marimon Cook house was donated by B. J. Shanower and moved to the Geauga County Historical Society, the land and farm were donated to Kent State University for a regional campus. The outside of the building is not photogenic.

The fee for an undergraduate is $90.75 per credit hour, an increase of $16.00 per credit hour. Graduate hours are $117.00 per credit hour, and a non-Ohio resident pays $182.75 per credit hour.

Associate degrees are given in business management technology, business administration, computer technology, technical study, and arts and science. Regular bachelor's degrees are only conferred by the main campus in Kent, Ohio. The final two years of study must be done there.

Seventeen courses were offered for the Summer Session, June 12 through August 5, 1989, ranging from art history to intuitive calculus.

There are many computer related courses at all sessions. An attempt is made to meet the needs of the community. There are classroom teacher workshops, desk-top publishing, programming, record keeping, and many others.
Courtesy of Kent State University, Geauga Campus

Dr. Larry D. Jones began his service early in the spring semester of 1987 and is the fifth dean since the campus opened during the spring of 1976. He replaced Joanne Fagerburg whose husband accepted a church in Connecticut.
Courtesy of Larry Jones

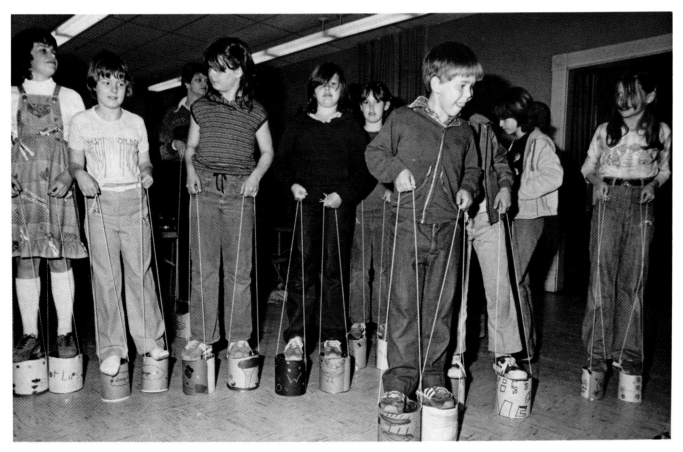

Learning comes in many forms as these children try out tin can stilts which they made during a craft session at Burton Public Library.
Courtesy of the Geauga Times Leader

Teaching and learning are not confined to a classroom. Field trips are carefully arranged to fit the curriculum. Here Doris Cook showed off The Times Leader *newspaper office and explained how the paper is written, pasted up, and printed to a group of second graders from Maple Elementary School in Chardon who toured the office in October 1979.*

The newspaper is no longer printed in Chardon. It is a tri-county operation involving Geauga, Lake, and Ashtabula Counties, and is printed in Ashtabula.
Courtesy of the Geauga Times Leader

Photograph by Marilyn Whipkey, courtesy of the Geauga Times Leader

Waiting to board the four-man chair lift at Alpine Valley are skiers of all sizes. The lifts carry skiers to the summit of one of the five hills at the Munson Township ski lodge. The winter of 1982 was especially good for advocates of the sport. The winter of 1988–1989 was one of the poorest for skiers (good for driveways, however).

Skiing certainly has become popular, thanks to the people at Alpine Valley. Local schools have made arrangements for skiing classes, and local recreation boards have worked with Alpine Valley to provide group consideration for classes and passes.

IN THE BULB THERE IS A FLOWER

CHAPTER 5

Farming has been by necessity a cooperative venture; neighbors helped each other. Farmers had support groups before it became "the thing" as Farmer's Clubs were very common.

The minutes of the meetings of some of the groups were published regularly. In this way the word could be spread to anyone who had access to the paper. The discussion would be on one theme, and each farmer could give his experiences for the edification of the others.

An organization called the Grangers was founded in 1867 for social and educational purposes. The National Grange of the Patrons of Husbandry, an American agrarian movement, became political forums as the farmers protested against economic abuses of the time. Through political activity, the Grangers were successful in promoting the concept of public regulation of private utilities devoted to public use. Other interested parties took up the issues, and the Grangers eventually relapsed into being social organizations again.

A. B. C. Chamberlain of Hambden was an active Granger, and this led to his becoming Worthy Deputy Master of Geauga County Granges. In that capacity he was the installing officer at the organization of Munson Grange 1549 on October 4, 1901, with nineteen charter members; the Newbury Grange on February 16, 1902, with twenty-nine charter members; and Huntsburg Grange 1588, in August 1903 with twenty charter members.

In 1885, David Miller of Holmes County hitched up his faithful buggy horse and started north, probably following the general direction of what is today Route 44. He was in search of cheaper land than that available in Holmes County. He found it in Geauga County. While his was not the first Amish family to move here, he was the first to come here.

The Amish settled in almost every township, but now their numbers are concentrated in the townships of Parkman, Middlefield, Troy, Burton, Huntsburg, and Claridon.
Courtesy of the Geauga Times Leader

The Ohio Cooperative Extension Service celebrated the 75th anniversary of its formation in May 1989. The office has been in various locations, mostly in Burton, and now shares the left half of the Patterson Center in Burton. From the brochure prepared for the anniversary: "You ask us about farming, homemaking, and youth. But today we have other answers, too.

 You've changed and so have we.
 We know what's ailing your azaleas.
 We know how to help you plan your lifestyle.
 We know how to get new businesses to your community.
 We know about genetic engineering and new food products.
 We know how to develop your youngster's leadership skills.

Ask us. We're the Ohio Cooperative Extension Service. We have the answers."

The 4-H (Head, Heart, Health, Hands) motto is "To Make the Best Better." The Geauga 4-H Clubs have members from farms, towns, urban centers, and all races and economic backgrounds. 4-H is alive and growing as their participation at the Great Geauga County Fair shows.

The right half of the Patterson Center in Burton is occupied by a Soil and Water Conservation District (SWCD) which is responsible for the conservation of soil and water resources within its boundaries. The services provided are:

 Maps of soil interpretations and land capability,
 Plans for design, layout, construction, and maintenance of conservation and pollution abatement practices,
 Assistance in the development and implementation of urban sediment control programs,
 Plans for the design and construction of water management systems and practices for erosion control, pollution abatement, flood protection, and water supply for domestic, recreational, and fire prevention purposes, and
 Assistance in planting and managing forests and wildlife food and shelter areas.

This question was posed to Evelyn Blair of Newbury Township, "What is the biggest change that you have seen in agriculture since the last history in 1953?"

Evelyn replied that regulations, equipment, disease, feeding, and management have all caused so many changes that it would have meant almost starting over. Evelyn and her husband Audre put in the first milking parlor in 1953 and sold the dairy in 1956.

AMISH IN GEAUGA COUNTY, OHIO

Historically, the Amish are direct descendants of the Anabaptists, a religious and social group which emerged from the Reformation in Central Europe about 1523. Differences over procedures and discipline resulted in the splintering off of numerous independent branches. One of these groups, called the Old Mennonites, was named for Menno Simons. Another Mennonite branch became the Amish Church led by Jakob Ammonn who left the parent group in Germany in the late 1600's and gave the new church its name. The Amish Mennonites began coming to the United States late in the seventeenth century, settling first in Pennsylvania, then in Ohio, and in other parts of the Middle West.

The first Amishman to settle in Geauga was Sam Weaver. In the spring of 1886, he and his family moved to a farm north of Parkman on State Route 528. David Miller moved to Geauga in 1887.

By 1902, the Amish population was estimated to be 1,500 with families in every township but Chardon. In an article in *The Plain Dealer* (Cleveland) on Sunday, December 23, 1984, Middlefield was ranked as having the second largest concentration of Amish in Ohio, behind Holmes County. Many Amish families are moving away because they feel that Middlefield has too many temptations for their teenagers.

The Amish do not view the automobile as wicked but they will not own one. The elders believe it will trend toward breakdown of the family unit, and hence the basic structure of the community. They will ride in taxicabs, and many a "Yankee" makes a living transporting Amish to work in factories and homes.

Many of the Mennonites in the area were once Old Order Amish and have left that faith. Mennonites are more liberal in that they do own automobiles and have and use electrical appliances. Their dress is

This gristmill in Parkman Township ground grain for farmers all over the "Reserve."

Three basic concerns faced the pioneer to Geauga County in the early 1800s; food, shelter, and clothing. The head of the family might have come the year before the move and cleared the land to plant grain.
Courtesy of Shetler Printing/Roose Drug

and Amish do not have business dealings with each other.

AGRICULTURAL STATISTICS—1987

A news release in the *Geauga Times Leader,* Thursday, April 13, 1989, by the Ohio Department of Taxation showed that Geauga County ranked twentieth from the bottom in total number of acres of agricultural property with 62,455 acres at a current agricultural use value of $4.6 million. The figures were based on the calendar year 1987.

Geauga County has 1,470 parcels of agricultural property. Their value at "highest and best use," or non-agricultural, would be $29.5 million.

All of the figures are taxable value, after the imposition of the 35 percent assessment ratio.

Gristmills and sawmills were often built at the same time, and water supplied the power. When pioneers selected their land, the water source was of extreme importance. Many a millrace and/or dam was washed out when a "freshet" rose.

The mill in Parkman operated by this source was destroyed by an arsonist in September 1967. It had been in full operation until the year before when Narvie Moss, the owner, retired.
Courtesy of Shetler Printing/Roose Drug

Hymn of Promise
by Natalie Sleeth
In the bulb, there is a flower;
In the seed, an apple tree;
In cocoons, a hidden promise:
Butterflies will soon be free!
In the cold and snow of winter
There's a Spring that waits to be,
Unrevealed until its season,
Something God alone can see.

Wade Leaman shows a display of flower and vegetable seeds for gardens.
Courtesy of Geauga Times Leader

Jay Gerlach, of Auburn, takes Pat and Mike, his oxen, to various events at the Geauga County Historical Society and uses them to pull a wagon which seats about fifteen children at a time.

Oxen were extensively used in the settlement and development of Geauga County. They were stronger and less flighty than horses.
Courtesy of the Geauga County Historical Society

One of the oldest landmarks of the county is found in the southwest part of Bainbridge. The old mill was built in 1820 by Gen. Chauncey Eggleston and Sanford Baldwin, two early pioneers. Baldwin sold out to Eggleston who ran the mill for more than thirty years, when he sold out to James Fuller. Fuller ran the mill until 1879 when failing health and the death of his wife caused him to abandon the business. James Fuller was born October 1, 1807, and died April 10, 1909. Cynthia, his wife, died May 13, 1879, aged fifty-seven years. Both are buried in Restland Cemetery in Bainbridge Township.
Courtesy of the The Geauga Republican, Wednesday, August 9, 1905

The temperature on Monday, January 11, 1982, had been frigid, but these draft horses had heavy winter coats to insulate against icy winds. They nuzzled each other's nose for enjoyment rather than for warmth. They were seen frolicking in the snow on an Auburn farm along State Route 44.

There are several species of draft horses; these are probably Belgians. Belgians are smaller and less expensive to keep.

Once a month, the Amish and "Yankees" enjoy a horse-pulling competition "to toughen the horses" on a farm in the Middlefield/Parkman area. Photography by Deborah Sekerak, Courtesy of the Geauga Times Leader

Captain Reese, Thomas Williams, and Will Nutt are shocking oats on the Williams farm in Russell. In the background is a binder which cuts the oats and ties them into bundles. The oats are hauled to a threshing machine which has been set up on the farm. The thresher might be owned by one person or several and travels with a crew to neighborhood farms. Threshing is a cooperative venture for both the men and women. The host farm is responsible for feeding the crew, and this is where the women "shine." There is a spirit of competition as to who has the best pies (and other foods) for the crew.
Courtesy of Richard Childs

Perry Cragg (1894–1970) is surrounded by a few of his photographs. He was a newspaper photographer in Cleveland for more than forty years.

Many of his photographs of the Amish (including the two at the right and the two on the bottom) were published in a book The Amish in 1971 as a fulfillment of his last wish. The book was reprinted in June 1989 by the Middlefield Cheese House.
Courtesy of Doris (Millard) Cragg

The Threshermen's Convention is an annual event held in August at Century Village in Burton. Spectators are watching as the steam engine chugs along pulling a wagon load of passengers.

A crew of three is required just to operate the steam engine when grain is threshed. A water monkey sees that the supply of water to the boiler is constant and that there is sufficient water to keep the engine cool. The engineer is in charge of the working parts of the engine which have to be lubricated every hour or so. The separator is in charge of setting up the operation and seeing that the engine and thresher are level, etc.

An eight-inch heavy canvas belt connects the main pulley of the threshing machine to the flywheel of the steam engine. The rest of the crew deal with bringing the sheaves of grain to the thresher and taking care of the end products; the straw and bags of grain. (from Ellis Wellman)

In this area, a crew of ten can thresh about eight hundred bushels of grain a day. Most of the bundle pitchers, baggers,

teamsters, etc., were the farmers in the area who helped each other. The farmers' wives worked together to feed the crew. It didn't take long for the men to find out where they would get the best biscuits, bread, or pies.
Courtesy of the Geauga County Historical Society

Clifford Burton, Sr., is whetting a scythe on a foot-powered whetstone on his farm one mile south and one mile west of Huntsburg Center. While this is September 1953, the scythe is still important in mowing and trimming areas that are not accessible to large tools. Duke, the dog, is obviously a great help.

The scythe would not have been used to cut the corn. That would have been done with a short, straight-handled corn knife. The corn has been husked and stored in the granary. The stalks are bunched and ready to be used for feed for the pigs, horses, and cows.
Photograph by Perry Cragg, Courtesy of Violet Warren

Flax is being spun in a demonstration at a festival at the Historical Society. This is one-half of a coarse material called linsey-woolsey. The stems have to be soaked or "ret" to cause the fibers to soften so that they can be separated. The seeds of flax are used for linseed oil.

"Every farmer had to have his quarter or half acre of flax to be worked up into cloth for the use of the family. As my memory carries me back to the days of my boyhood, those long ago days, I can well remember the feeling of spite I used to have toward that piece of flax all the time it was growing, for I well knew that on lowery days in haying, when I wanted to go fishing, I should have to stay at home and pull flax." (from J. C. Wells, "The Old Agricultural Society," 1898.)
Courtesy of the Geauga County Historical Society

The other half of linsey-woolsey is walking around in this scene from a postcard. Many of the settlers came from Connecticut where it is said about Hartland that the sheep had sharp noses so that they could graze between the stones and rocks.

During the night of March 10, 1989, four ewes and their nursing lambs, all about two months old, were killed on the farm of Ed and Judy (Hunt) Ward in Claridon Township. By Saturday evening, four more died. The animals that were killed were part of a flock of about thirty white Suffolk sheep. Ward estimated that the value of the twelve animals was about twelve hundred dollars. The consensus of opinion was that coyotes were the predators because the wounds were around the head and throat. Dogs tend to attack hindquarters.

The Wards sell some of the lambs once they are weaned to 4-H children who in turn use the animals as club projects. Some of them are exhibited at the Great Geauga County Fair.
Courtesy of Virginia Hyde

This store in Middlefield in the early 1900s dealt in farm implements. On the right is a mower. The concept of the mower has not changed very much except that the mowing knife is powered by a tractor. On the left is a grinding wheel, an important item in keeping the mowing knife sharpened.

A knife is made up of triangular-shaped sections (about three-and-one-half inches on each side) sharpened on two sides. Thus, if one section broke, it could be easily replaced.

In back of the dealer is a hay loader. It is hitched to the back of a wagon and brings the hay or straw from a windrow to load on the wagon.
Courtesy of Shetler Printing/Roose Drug

R. C. Grosvenor, Harrison Rowley, Julius Kleinfeld, and other farmers pooled their resources to buy a combine. The combine did what its name denotes; it combined the operations of cutting the grain and binding it into shocks, stacking the shocks, hauling the shocks to the threshing machine set up in the barnyard, and taking care of the grain.

In one operation, the grain was cut, threshed, and deposited into bags. When the bag was filled, a miller's knot was applied, and the bag was placed on the sloped platform. When the combine reached the end of the field, a trip released the bags into a pile to be picked up later.
Courtesy of June Kellogg

Holstein cows rest, graze, and chew their cuds. Most Amish herds are Holsteins because the production of milk is higher, although the milk isn't as high in butterfat as Jerseys or Guernseys.
Photo by Perry Cragg, courtesy of Doris Cragg

The corn planter is making short work of planting corn seed. The arm to the right is marking out a guide for the return trip. A trench is dug, treated seed and fertilizer are dropped at spaced intervals, and the machine covers the seed—a far cry from the Pilgrims' method of digging the hole and burying a fish with the seed.
Courtesy of Patterson Center

An old-fashioned barn raising was held at the Geauga County Historical Society Pioneer Village in Burton during the summer of 1975.

The barn had been taken down piece by piece, section by section in 1973 from the B. J. Shanower farm north of Burton and moved to the historical museum property.

Preliminary work was begun on Thursday and Friday by a handful of men so that all was in readiness on Saturday. Mrs. Clara Yoder headed up a committee of women for serving an Amish-Dutch lunch to the volunteer workers. The main meal would include a meat (chicken or a roast), mashed potatoes and gravy, and vegetables. Pie was a staple, and there were other rich desserts. A meal prepared by the Amish at the Historical Society usually included seven-layer salad, Amish bread, and apple butter.
Courtesy of the Geauga Times Leader

The silo filler is powered by a belt. Corn stalks are fed into the device which chops the stalks and blows the silage up the pipe on the outside of the silo. The shocks are brought from the field on a wagon and fed into the machine. Many a worker has lost a hand or arm from getting caught in a silo filler.

A worker inside the silo moves the feed pipe around so that the silo is evenly filled.
Courtesy of Shetler Printing/Roose Drug

Helen Novak and Helen Coats show visitors to a festival at the Geauga County Historical Society the art of churning cream to make butter. Many factors contribute to the success of butter making. The temperature of both the atmosphere and the cream, the quantity of cream, the speed at which the crank is turned, the humidity, etc., all have to be considered.

A two-gallon glass churn was mounted on a Shopsmith (a combination saw, drill press, planer, lathe, etc., with a variable speed option). The paddles were removed from the lid and mounted in the drill press. The butter "gathered" in eight to ten minutes. With the hand method and less than ideal conditions, the process would sometimes take half a day.
Courtesy of the Geauga County Historical Society

After the butter gathered, the buttermilk would be poured off and used for drinking and cooking. Then the process of washing the butter would begin. Emma Baumgartner is using the familiar wooden bowl and paddle. A good washing job takes several changes of water to get all the buttermilk out. When the water doesn't turn milky, the job is done. The butter washings were saved for the pigs. The excess water left in the butter has to be squeezed out with the paddle. Then salt is worked into the butter at the discretion of the homemaker. The butter is packed in crocks and kept as cool as possible.
Courtesy of the Geauga County Historical Society

The Apple Butter Festival is held on the second weekend of October on the grounds of the Geauga County Historical Society in Burton. Mrs. John Bican, Mrs. Maria McLaughlin, and Jessie Dutton are faced with the formidable task of peeling all those apples. While the ladies have volunteered to help with the festival, this chore was a common occurrence in all households in getting the food supply ready for the long winter.
Courtesy of the Geauga County Historical Society

Frank Samuel carries the kettles used for making apple butter. The pared apples have been quartered and the core removed. Water is added (a minimum quantity), and the mixture is cooked until the apples are mushy. Tending the fire and stirring frequently would keep a homemaker busy. Sugar and spices such as cinnamon, cloves, and ginger are added. Then the cooking and stirring begins in earnest. The thicker and darker it becomes, the better the taste.
Courtesy of the Geauga County Historical Society

When Geauga County was first settled, it was noted that a squirrel could travel from Lake Erie to the Ohio River and never touch the ground. In 1979, State Farm Forester Ture Johnson fixed up a Division of Forestry booth at the Geauga County Fair in Burton. Ture has since retired but still lends his expertise to Syrup Producers' meetings, nursery associations, etc. Many farms in Geauga are designated tree farms because of Ture's efforts.

The Ohio Federation of Soil and Water Conservation Districts has an office at the Patterson Center in Burton. For some thirty years, various kinds of seedlings have been made available for pick-up and planting during April. A newsletter called The Geaugrapher began in 1979. The issue mailed in January advertises the various packets and gives ordering information. The 1989 Tree Packet program had the following varieties: Packet A contained eight nut trees, two each of four varieties; Packet B was a Flowering Tree Packet of ten trees (five varieties); Packet C had twenty-five Blue Spruce seedlings; Packet D had twenty-five Scotch Pines; and Packet E had twenty-five crowns of Crownvetch. The first four packets were ten dollars each, and Crownvetch cost six dollars. The order blank had helpful hints such as "Best in full sun" (Scotch Pine) and "Does not like wet soil" (Blue Spruce). The seedlings come from out of state, mostly Pennsylvania and Michigan. None are grown locally.
Courtesy of the Geauga Times Leader

The Williams Farm on Fairmount Road in Russell Township has been in the family several generations. Robert Williams is deceased, but his wife Laurita still lives in the house. Most of the land is rented for crops.

Farmers take a great deal of pride in the appearance of the property. Straight corn rows would show a passer-by how careful the farmer was.
Courtesy of Richard Childs

The Domestic Hall is one of the oldest buildings on the Fairgrounds. An association styled "The Geauga County Agricultural and Manufacturing Society" came as a result of the meeting held at Chardon, January 15, 1823, and the first fair or exhibition held by the Society was at Chardon, October 23, 1823.

By 1849, it was evident that permanent grounds were needed. Proposals were received from Chardon, Claridon, and Burton. Burton's proposition received the majority of votes at the annual meeting of the Society and was accepted. A tract of eleven acres north of the Public Square was leased from H. H. Ford. The grounds were fenced, a track fifty rods in circuit was graded and a railing built around it, and a suitable hall and stand were built. The whole amount paid by the Society for fitting up the grounds, building the hall, etc. was $1078.68.
(from J. C. Wells, "The Old Agricultural Society," 1898)
Courtesy of the Geauga Times Leader

The original grandstand at the Burton Fairgrounds had its back to North Cheshire Street, and the racetrack was in the area where farm machinery is displayed. Note the interurban track in the lower left hand corner.

Pickpockets were a definite hazard at the fair. They would get off the streetcar and say, "The pickpockets are out." The farmers would slap their hip pockets to check for wallets, and this gave the pickpockets the location. Finally detectives were hired to see that the pickpockets took the next car back to town.
Courtesy of Sylvia Wiggins

These horsemen are probably leading the parade at the Century Fair of 1931 at Burton. From left to right are: Stanlae Merritt, Art Thrasher, Ben Owen, Ford Hosmer, and Pleman Gharky.

The parade and pageant were held to commemorate the first fair which apparently the committee thought was in 1831. By the time the 1953 history was published, the mistake had been corrected. The first fair was held in Chardon in 1823. The fair of 1988 was billed as the 165th meeting.
Courtesy of Isabel Jamieson

Decked out in their best are G. B. and Lottie (Doolittle) Fox in the back seat and Fred and Ellen (?) Talcott in the front. They are participating in the Century Fair of 1931 parade riding in an oxen-drawn, two-wheel cart. No one is driving the oxen; they are being guided by the teamster whose place is at the head of the oxen.
Courtesy of Isabel Jamieson

The Great Geauga County Fair Band performs at the 1982 Fair. Their uniforms are two-tone blue; the weather decides whether jackets are worn. Left front are Jan Stewart and T. Dwight Ladd, flautists.

The whole idea for a fair band began in 1937 by Azro M. Cheney and Cliff Rossiter of Chardon. It primarily started to give high school seniors and those people out of school an opportunity to continue their musical skills. The band project caught on, and 1938 fairgoers heard what was to become a tradition.

The Great Geauga County Fair Band celebrated its 50th anniversary at the fair in 1988. There were still four charter members playing with the band: Barbara Ricca, Betty Palmer, Vernon Howard, and T. Dwight Ladd. Each received a plaque from the band and a certificate presented by Congressman Dennis Eckart. Fair Board President Kenneth Kronk read a letter of commendation to the entire band.
Courtesy of the Geauga Times Leader

Starr Quality Produce is still sold at this farm stand on Mayfield Road in Claridon Township. The present owner, Donald Starr, is the fourth generation owner.

The spring crop consists of flower and vegetable seedlings. The Claridon Township Trustees order over two hundred geraniums for decorating the graves of veterans of all the wars. During the summer, the stand has strawberries, tomatoes, squash, onions, and other vegetables. During October, the front yard has a mound of pumpkins. In December, Christmas trees and decorating boughs are sold.

HALF A MAN

For forty years
I've worked this land.
It's nurtured my dreams
And calloused my hand.
I've loved it for its beauty
That transcends all seasons,
For the grain, the corn, the hay, the wood,
Generosity, among other reasons.

Over the years,
It happened so gradually,
This land
Became a part of me.
To see its rolling hills
Scarred by giant metal towers
Would be the beginning of the end.
Painful to me
As the death of a friend.

If the day should ever come
When the rustle of the leaves
Cannot be heard
For the crackle and hum,
I'd only be
Half a man
If power lines
Divide my land.
    Anonymous

UP WITH PEOPLE POWER; DOWN WITH TOWER POWER. This was the logo for the fight of hundreds of Geauga citizens against Cleveland Electric Illuminating Company who wanted to build transmission lines from the Perry Nuclear Power Plant through the heart of Geauga County to hook into a grid system in Portage County. The proposed route went through prime agricultural land, parks and preserves, wetlands, and residential areas.

The fight began in late February and early March of 1982 at the Claridon Town Hall. An organization, the Geauga Preservation Society, was formed. Andrea Pollock of Claridon and representatives from seven affected townships made up the Board. Andrea was and still is the Chairperson. It would be impossible to name all those who donated time and money. Thousands of dollars were raised to pay for expert witnesses, legal fees, and other expenses.

The fight ended (at least temporarily) on June 3, 1985, when the Ohio Power Siting Board rejected the proposed line as not needed. It was official on September 20, 1985, when the time for CEI to file an appeal expired. The end is temporary because CEI could change the proposed route/routes slightly and start all over again.

Courtesy of GEAUGANSPEAK, Bulletin Forty-four, March 1986

NATURE IS SWEET

CHAPTER 6

This storage tank was one of two built in the 1870s by John Flavel Grosvenor and was in constant use until it was retired to the Jonathan Hale Farm of the Western Reserve Historical Society in January 1989. The capacity is about five hundred gallons. A yardstick was the gauge for how hot to have the fire and when to start shutting down. When the measurement was five inches deep, it was time to slow down because the remaining fire would finish the job overnight.

The new building in the background replaced the "sap room" which held the two tanks (and not much else). The older part of the building in the upper right corner has doors which are opened when boiling is being done so that the steam can escape.

The tank is sitting on the old roadway which is sloped. The horses (later tractor) would pull the sled or wagon up the slope. A pipe from the tank would be lowered into a metal trough (made from eave spouting), and sap would flow directly into the tank. A cloth bag was fastened over the end of the trough for straining bits of bark, etc.

A FANTASY

*I would seek again Geauga's wilds,
Their dangers again I'd dare;
Where the he-skunk howls,
And the rabbit growls,
And the wood-chuck makes his lair.*

*I'd follow again the awesome brook,
That leads to that dismal fen,
Where the fierce bullfrog,
From his home on the log,
Affrights the sons of men.*

*Yes, I would view those scenes again,
Those perils dare once more;
I'd meet the muskrat face to face,
Challenge the coon to mortal embrace,
Nor quail at the chipmunk's roar.*

*And if so be, that I should fall;
So be, that my blood be shed;
Oh lay me away,
In Geauga clay,
With a maple tree at my head.*
—anonymous
New York, April 1908

THE PRODUCTION OF SYRUP

Why is there sap? Sap is the food of the tree. All vegetation has to have food and in the trees, the moisture is sap. "The flow of sap is due to internal pressure produced by the more rapid expansion of the sap than the wood, the rise in temperature causing the expansion at a time when the tree is saturated with sap. The necessary saturation is helped by a period in which the roots are absorbing moisture from moist soil, while at the same time evaporation from the tree is checked by low temperatures." (From *Historical Society Quarterly*, April 1963)

The earliest indication of "sugar making" is dated 1814, in Burton, but could be as early as

1807. "They (Indians) made sugar on the flats southeast of Conant's, on the Hickox farm, towards the river. They had a fine 'bush' of large hard maples, on the field where James Humiston had corn in 1878. He plowed through the boiling places and turned up charred stone and wood." (From *Pioneer and General History of Geauga County . . ., 1880*, page 470)

"An interesting fact was discovered by A. C. Beales some years ago based on investigation of a fallen tree on his farm. A cross-section of the tree revealed 240 rings. Scars of previous tappings extended back to 120 rings, showing that the tree had been tapped first in 1812, the year his great-great-grandfather had come to Geauga. Each tapping leaves a scar of dead wood in the tree trunk which extends a foot or more above and below the site tapped. The first scars showed irregular notches for elder spouts, later a different type of hole, then ones made by augers and smaller bits." (From *Historical Society Quarterly*, April 1963)

Geauga County claims to have about half a million maples yielding sap this spring (From *The Geauga Republican*, Wednesday, April 3, 1870). All summer the same trees will beautify the Geauga hills and valleys. They will grow larger in trunk and bough, greater in stretch of shade. They will create more vegetation mold of the richest kind for the benefit of future generations. Their roots and leaves will help make the Geauga woods storehouses of moisture to feed springs and streams through the heat and possible drought of July and August.

DIARY OF CLINTON GOODWIN MAKING SYRUP 1867

About two miles north of the Newell/Grosvenor farm in Claridon was another farming operation. Clinton's wife Lucy was a daughter of Judge Lester Taylor, the originator of the Geauga County Historical Society. From Clinton Goodwin's diary:

Saturday, 16 Feb 1867   Tapped 6 trees.

According to legend, the Indian tapped the tree by chopping a hole with his tomahawk, letting the sap run into a hollow log.

The pioneer made spiles or spouts from elder branches and collected the sap in wooden buckets sometimes attaching four or five to a single tree.

The modern tapping method is a gas or battery powered drill.

Tuesday, 19 Feb   Chopped wood in woods afternoon.

Tremendous piles of wood are needed for the evaporation. The best wood was American chestnut, but it no longer exists. Hickory is excellent; maple and ash are good. Oak holds a fire for a long time, but it isn't flashy. Other fuels as coal, oil, and natural gas have been used with varying degrees of success. Nothing adds to the atmosphere of a sugar house more than the smell of a wood fire.

Sat., 23   Tapped few more trees and took logs to mill.

Mon., 25 Lester came up and helped hoop buckets.

Wooden buckets gave way to tin pails which rusted too easily. Galvanizing the pails was the next step. Plastic bags replaced metal pails. In many bushes, plastic tubing has become the collecting method of choice.

Tues., 26   Lester helped saw sugar wood and lift buckets.

Thurs., 28 Feb   Tapped 145 trees set pans and built chimney.

The evaporator of 1867 was far better than the open kettle. The IXL was sold by Henry Hill. It was shown at the Chicago Exposition in 1896.

Fri., 1 Mar   worked from 4 until 11 night get 11 bbls sap. 184 trees tapped.

Sat., 2 Mar   gathered 8 bbls sap and boiled in. Lester boiled until 11 night.

Gathering was first done by simply carrying the pails. A yoke helped ease the burden.

The next step was a gathering tank on a sled pulled by horses or oxen. It was not necessary to "drive" a good woods team. "Gee," "Haw," "Giddap," and "Whoa" were all the words needed for most of the way. As farms and woods became more mechanized, a tractor replaced the horses. The constant battle in the woods was mud. Even now, several years later, the scars of the ruts are still visible.

In 1983, the Grosvenor woods became the Pollock woods. With the advent of a closed

The mighty ax gave way to a modern way of supplying the inordinate amount of wood needed for a season. This splitter is powered by a power take-off on a tractor. The log is placed against the wedge to the left. The pressure of the ram drives the log into the wedge.

Sap is the food of the tree, and it is also a refreshing prelude to spring. These two young ladies sample some of the crystal clear, somewhat sweet liquid. The location is not identified, but it could have been anywhere in Geauga County and was probably taken in the mid 1890s. Courtesy of Shetler Printing/Roose Drug

vacuum tubing system, sap flows through main lines into a collecting tank. From there, the sap is pumped to the sugar house.

Mon., 4 (Mar) Snowy syruped off and brought down syrup. Loaded log.

Flat pans were raised to "syrup off."
The next improvement was to add flues or fins to the sap pans. This was to increase the boiling surface.

As the density of the liquid increases, it is pushed to the front pans by the flow of sap into the back pans. Syrup can be taken from the front pan, but a better method is to use a finishing pan where the heat can be better controlled.

The 1988-1989 season saw the introduction and use of reverse osmosis. With this method, 75 percent of the water is removed from the sap before it gets to the evaporator. One disadvantage of this method is that it is no longer possible to cook potatoes and eggs in the sap as it is much too sweet.

Tues., 5 Hauled two logs to mill and two loads lumber. Lester up here and we sugared off.
Sat., 9 Tapped 50 trees p.m. gathered 1 bbl sap.
Mon., 11 Lester & self gathered 11 bbls sap and boiled. I tapped some.
Tues., 12 Sugared off twice, gathered 2 bbls. 33 bbls up to this time.
Wed., 13 I syruped off, sudden change cold.
Fri., 15 Not well fixed up. 5 buckets.
Sat 23 Mar Gathered 10 bbls sap. 44 up to this time. Snow wet and heavy.
Mon., 25 Gathered 11 bbls sap. syruped off at 1 p.m.
Tues., 26 Up at 4 and boiled sap in by 1 p.m. Sugared off.
Sat., 30 Sugared off. Gathered 6 bbls sap. 61 up to this time.
Mon., 1 Apr Gathered sap & went to town meeting.
Tues., 2 Apr Finished gathering sap twenty bbls including what we got on Saturday.
Wed., 3 Went to woods put about 50 spiles in trees.
Thurs., 4 Gathering and boiling got 6 bbls. Broke my finger first thing.
Sat., 6 Gathered 4 bbls sap.

Mon., 8 Gathered 4 bbls sap and boiled in.
Tues., 9 Tapped over some trees.
Wed., 10 Gathered and boiled two bbls sap. rainy afternoon.
Sat., 13 Took up buckets and scalded them.

Buckets were washed at the beginning and end of each season.

Tubing is left up from one season to the next. A Clorox solution is pumped through the tubing to wash it.

Clinton was careful to report how many barrels of sap he gathered, but he does not say how many gallons of syrup resulted. The worth of the season was measured by the proportion of barrels of sap to gallons of syrup. The "sweetest" year in the Grosvenor woods was one barrel to one gallon. An average year was about forty-two gallons of sap to one gallon of syrup.

There is no accurate measure with the reverse osmosis system as it is now. There are probably meters or gauges available that would measure the concentrate.

In the twenties, Geauga County was producing more maple syrup per square mile than any other part of the syrup producing belt. There were two thousand producers in the county. On a good day, a person could stand in the Claridon Center Cemetery and see the steam rising from sixteen bushes.

Burton has the only municipally owned and operated sugar camp on the North American continent. This sugar camp is operated wholly under the auspices of the Burton Chamber of Commerce.

During the maple syrup season, the quaint old log cabin in the park will be seen nearly encircled by travelers' cars from far and near.

THE MAPLE FESTIVAL

Arthur Carlson, a Chardon hardware dealer, came up with the idea of a festival in order to promote the syrup market. The first one was in 1926 with an estimated attendance of two thousand. Another account said that "Chardon was besieged by ten thousand visitors during the two-day event."

In 1927, the festival ended with a balance of $92.03 in the savings account. It was cancelled in

1980 because of a short sap run and was not held for two years during World War II. The Festival of 1989 was the 60th Anniversary of the first event.

To promote an early festival, a contest was held. The verses of T. Dwight Ladd of Claridon were declared the best. Musicians then competed to put the verses to music. This was won by James Quentin Thrasher.

CHARDON

MAPLE SUGAR CENTER OF THE WORLD

Words by T. Dwight Ladd

Music by James Q. Thrasher

Published by Chardon Civic Association,

Chardon, Ohio.
Copyright 1929 by James Q. Thrasher
Dedicated to THE CHARDON KIWANIS CLUB

1. Look-ing from her hill top, O'er the country side,
   Wind-ing roads and wood-lands
   Fields and meadows wide,
   Sits our lit-tle cit-y Bathed in sunlight glow,
   Fair-est of the Buck-eye towns Char-don O-hi-o.
CHORUS
2. In the earl-y spring-time, King Ma-ple rules su-preme,
   And the streets of Chardon With throngs of peo-ple teem,
   Fair or storm-y weath-er Sun-shine rain or snow,
   All high ways lead to Ma-ple-dom at Chardon O-hi-o.

CHORUS
3. A sign of hope and pro-gress to all the coun-try side,
   The flow-er of the Berk-shires And old Ge-au-gas pride,
   The home of hap-py peo-ple Who've learned that here be-low,
   The near-est thing to heav'n on earth is Chardon O-hi-o.
CHORUS
   O Char-don, dear old Char-don, Your prais-es we will sing,
   Un-til the fields and for-ests, With ech-oes loud-ly ring.
   Go search the wide world o-ver, But as for us we know
   The fair-est spot is home sweet home in Char-don O-hi-o.

In 1962, attendance was estimated at 120,000 visitors.

The 1989 Festival was the 60th because a festival was not held during World War II. The Festival Parade was dedicated to Karen Dufur who had served as festival president for several years. She died February 4, 1989.

Early syrup makers never had the comforts of home. This sugar house was constructed from a dismantled wood silo in the early 1940s. The outside is barn red.

This is a display of the various kinds of spiles used. All but the two at the top are metal. The ones for tubing are plastic and are called spouts.

Tapping the trees meant that a 3/8" or 7/16" diameter hole, about 3" deep, was drilled. A pellet containing paraformaldehyde was inserted before a spile was carefully pounded into the hole. The chemical slows bacterial growth which would stop the flow of sap. When the season ends, any residue in the hole should be flushed out.

A bucket was hung on the spile and a metal cover was put on the bucket. For a right-handed person, the cover was placed so that the gatherer had only to tip up the bucket to pour out the sap into a gathering pail.

The Indians would gash the maple tree to start the sap flow which was collected in a hollow log. The first spiles were made from a piece of elderberry, buckthorn sumac, or sassafras. All have a soft center which had to be removed.

Occasionally, the woods would be retapped using a cane spile just above the metal spile. The quality of the syrup at that point in the season was fair to poor. Many operators felt that it wasn't worth it. At best, it was a gamble as to what the production would be.
Courtesy of Richards Maple Products

This wooden gathering tank is on display at Richards Maple Products in Chardon. When a load was brought to the sugar house, the sap had to be dipped out and poured into a storage tank.

If this wooden bucket were handmade today, the cost would be far more than twenty dollars. The wood would dry out from one season to the next. Soaking the bucket in water would expand the wood so that little sap was wasted. The hoops often had to be tightened.
Courtesy of Richards Maple Products

The quality of syrup took a giant step forward when the evaporator was invented. This was a model demonstrated at the World's Columbian Exposition in Chicago in 1892 by Henry Hill. "Syruping off" meant checking the consistency of the syrup and then raising the front pan using a rope and pulley arrangement.

Geauga County won first prize for maple syrup at the Exposition. The syrup was made on the H. N. Ensign farm in Claridon by James Ensign, a son, then ten years of age, who "boiled down" the sap while his father gathered it. The prize was a bronze medal which bore a likeness of Christopher Columbus and was appropriately inscribed. That quart of syrup still existed in 1933 at the home of James Ensign in Akron.
Courtesy of Sylvia Wiggins

This closed ring, water cooled vacuum pump is at the sugar house, one-half mile from the collecting tanks. The five-horsepower pump provides the suction to bring the sap from the trees to the collecting tanks. It is capable of operating over four thousand taps.

A syrup producer does not have a ready answer to, "How many trees do you tap?" The answer is in taps, not trees. When spiles and buckets were used, it was easy to count at the end of the season during clean-up.

Some producers put a "pill" in the hole as soon as it is drilled. So the answer to how many taps was the number of pills that were used.

The pill retards the growth of bacteria, but it also slows down the natural healing of the tree at the end of the season.

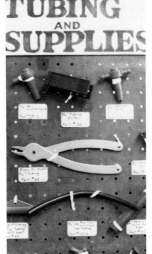

These are the tools needed to work with tubing. The special pliers in the middle are used to stretch the tubing to fit over the spouts and various connectors.

During the season, there is constant vigilance for leaks. Many of these are caused by squirrels looking for the sweet liquid. The tubing is not taken down at the end of the season. It is thoroughly washed with a solution of bleach and water.
Photograph by Teeter Grosvenor, courtesy of Richards Maple Products

In later models of evaporators, the pan is not raised. The current trend is to "take off" a batch before it is quite "ready" and complete the process in a finishing pan.

This "Waterloo" has several features designed to make it more efficient. One feature is a network of copper pipes suspended above the flue pans. The cold concentrate is heated by the steam rising from the boiling process so that by the time the concentrate is released into the "rig" the sap is already quite warm.

Along with a plumbing degree, an engineering degree would be useful to read these various dials and know when to open or close one of umpteen valves.

This is a primitive maple camp that was erected for an early festival.

Sugaring off was not a daily event. Since it takes over forty gallons of sap to make one gallon of syrup and the pans weren't big enough, sap was almost constantly added. The finished product was very dark.

Using reverse osmosis, about ten gallons of syrup were produced per hour in the Pollock woods during the 1989 season.
Courtesy of the Geauga County Historical Society

This is a side view of a reverse osmosis device or "R.O." The room is small and heated. It helps to have a degree in plumbing to understand how to put this all together. "The olden days" were much simpler.

Reverse osmosis is a way to remove 75 percent of the water from the sap. The process uses membranes to accomplish the task. The membranes must be kept clean, and much of the distilled water produced in the process is used. The R.O. must not be allowed to freeze, so a gas heater was installed.

The finishing pan is equipped with a thermometer which must be calibrated at least once a boiling day. Syrup must be seven degrees above the boiling point of distilled water to meet the standard of eleven pounds per gallon. When the proper temperature is reached, the syrup is pumped through the pressure filter.

From the finishing pan, the next step is the pressure filter. There is a great deal of wood silica in the finished product which must be removed. Formerly, the syrup was strained through cloth and felt strainers.

"Solomon (Johnson) Sr. was left handed and is the only Johnson I ever knew with this trait. He was a man of short temper and thin patience, and many stories were told by my father of the quick and often impulsive things he used to do with that trusty left. One story in particular shows what happened when things didn't move just right or as fast as he thought they should. He was straining syrup in the sugar bush with my father holding the strainer. The syrup, boiled in the old open kettle was as usual pretty thick with ashes and other foreign matter and was going through too slow to suit the old man, and in a flash he out with his old 'chicken caller' knife and with that good left hand stabbed holes in the strainer and said, 'Now I guess it will run.' He was a hard working man and a good neighbor and held the respect of the community."

A hose from the filter goes into a drum. Depending on the grade of syrup, it is pumped to a canning tank or put in drums for bulk sales. (From Geauga County Historical Society, Johnson File)

Producers hauled drums of syrup to a dealer in Middlefield (along Route 87) in the early 1900s.

Trucks replaced horses for all but Amish producers. Now Paul Richards goes to their farms (and some Yankee bushes) and picks up drums of syrup using a special lift at the back of the truck. The net weight of a thirty-gallon drum of syrup would be 330 pounds.
Courtesy of Shetler Printing/Roose Drug

"Hi, there, ye gol durn brute! Come down from there! Where d'ye think ye're going? I say, get out o' that elevator! Whoa! Back! Look out! Ye're tipping out all the surrip." (Clipping from Marian Bottger who said that it was probably from a Cleveland newspaper in 1903.)

Harlan Page Green, of South Newbury, had brought a wagon load of maple syrup to town (Cleveland), and when he drove into the alley behind Chandler and Rudd's he thought the elevator post was a good place to hitch his horse while he went in to dicker his "biled down sap." Everything would have been all right if somebody on the third floor hadn't wanted the elevator.
Courtesy of Richard Childs

Special runs were made by the interurban to visit a sugar bush. This car was on the Chagrin Falls Line and had stopped at Bell Road near Route 44 according to A. Piper. A member of the Christiansen family, on the other hand, said that the stop was closer to Burton.

"Many autos never reach the Festival due to heavy highway traffic congestion." The National Railway Historical Society and the Baltimore & Ohio Railroad organized a "safe, comfortable trip" to the Maple Festival on Sunday, April 12, 1953. A train left Canton at 8:30 a.m. and stopped in Akron, Kent, Ravenna, Newton Falls, and Warren. The fare from Canton was four dollars for adults; children were half fare. The train left Chardon at 5:00 p.m.
Courtesy of Anderson Allyn

The first log cabin erected in the Public Square of Burton was built in 1931 and was used for making syrup until 1961 when fire ruined the inside. If the only steam exit was the small round pipe at the left, it must have been impossible to see what was going on inside.
Courtesy of the Geauga County Historical Society

The first customer at the new (and much larger) Log Cabin in Burton (built in 1961) is Frank Fiegle. From left to right: Garland Shetler, Maurice Fox, Frank Fiegle, and Hilda Hosmer.
Courtesy of the Geauga County Historical Society

William S. and Rena Richards are shown at a display of their products. The Richards family has been in Geauga County since 1816 when Austin Richards came. His great-great-grandson, William S., became the founder of Richards Maple Products in 1910.

At the World's Fair in Chicago in July 1933, the Quaker Oats Company was demonstrating a pancake flour and were serving three cakes and a small carton of Vermont maple syrup for a dime. W. S. Richards had been having his breakfast there and remarked that he could furnish better syrup. The result was that Richards got an order for one thousand gallons. He hurried back to Geauga on Saturday, July 8th, and on Monday was on his way back to Chicago with the order. In order to meet the demand, Richards offered Geauga operators seven cents a pound (seventy-seven cents per gallon) when most dealers were offering six cents a pound.
Courtesy of Paul Richards

Paul Richards was born into syrup and candy making. He bought the business when his father, William S., retired in 1963. Paul's beard is a festival tradition.

Paul needs about thirty thousand gallons of good syrup per year and makes twenty-five to thirty thousand pounds of candy. Fifty-six years saw the price paid for bulk syrup go from $.07 per pound paid in 1933 to $1.85 in 1989.
Courtesy of the Geauga Times Leader

These are maple sugar maple leaves and are priced at $4.94 for an eight ounce box if picked up in the store. The same box shipped to the far western states would be $7.66. Orders addressed to a post office box would be an additional $.60 for insurance.

For sugar candy, the syrup is boiled to 236 degrees. The hot liquid is stirred until milky in appearance and almost ready to set. It is then poured into molds. A variety of shapes are available.

David Rennie pours the hot stirred liquid into a rabbit mold. Three-fourths of a gallon of syrup was needed. This rabbit was made for the 1981 Maple Festival. It was nineteen and one-half inches tall and weighed approximately six pounds. A lamb was also made that weighed nine pounds and ten ounces. Antique tin molds owned by the Richards family which date back to the early 1920s were used for the designs.
Courtesy of Richards Maple Products

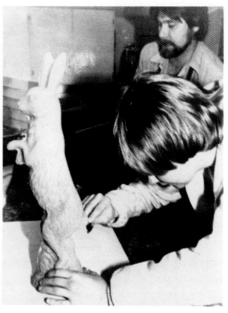

Mindy Meek, a candymaker for Richards Maple Products, used a sharp knife to scrape off the excess sugar on the rabbit. Courtesy of Richards Maple Products

An attempt was made to make the largest pure maple sugarcake to be entered in the Guiness Book of Records. The sugarcake took about six gallons of syrup, weighed forty five and three-fourths pounds (authenticated by the county auditor) and had a circumference at the base of four feet, five inches. The cake was put up for auction at the end of the festival.
Courtesy of Richards Maple Products

Various types of labels have been used on syrup cans. Time was when a paper label was pasted to a shiny can. Now lithographed tin cans can be ordered with all kinds of scenes (usually seasonally related). The cans are made in Solon, Ohio, by the Davies Can Company, but the distributor is located in Vermont. There are thirty-five gallon cans per case and are priced at $1.72 each when purchased by the case. Single gallon cans would be $1.77 each. Brown plastic jugs are $1.29 each by the case. However, jugs "breathe." If the syrup is stored in jugs for several months, the syrup will darken and there will be a slight change in flavor.

The syrup is canned hot and immediately sealed with an inner cap. The cans must have air space around them until they are cooled or stack burn will result. If the syrup is of the proper density and canned correctly, it will last many years. In one instance, a quart of syrup was sent to Alaska to a family member stationed there. The post office returned the can ten years later. When opened, the syrup was found to be almost as good as when it was made.
Courtesy of Richards Maple Products

Jennie Kaye served as a judge of maple products and open baking contests in the 1982 festival. The maple products competition is as old as the festival, but the baking contest didn't begin until 1977.

Categories for maple products include novel design, cream, pound sugar cake, one dozen small sugar cakes, and stirred sugar items.

There are no specific categories for the baking contest except that items have to be made with maple syrup and the recipe submitted with the entry.

Maple sugar is more a novelty now, but during most of the nineteenth century it was the only sweetening agent used in the kitchen.
Courtesy of the Geauga Times Leader

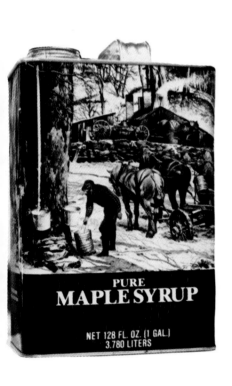

Cleveland's Randall Mall had a recreation and travel show during the first weekend in May 1980. The Geauga County Maple Festival Booth was one of twenty Ohio festivals represented there. The 1980 Maple Queen Allison Kozak and Maple Princess Kelly Stone (of Montville) confer with Festival Director Beverly Carver.
Photograph by Doris Cook, courtesy of the Geauga Times Leader

This group of children are probably on a field trip to the Chardon Maple Festival and are enjoying Maple Stir. Syrup is boiled to 234 degrees for maple cream. The syrup is poured carefully into a small dish and allowed to cool. Then stirring begins and continues until it is light and creamy.
Courtesy of the Geauga Times Leader

There are framed sketches of each of the recipients that hang in the Maple Syrup Hall of Fame located at the Patterson Center in Burton, Ohio. The sketch for Ralph Grosvenor was done from this polaroid shot taken at a niece's wedding in 1958. It is unfortunate that Belle Grosvenor was not included as she was the head of the sugar house and did at least 90 percent of the boiling.

The Maple Syrup Hall of Fame began in 1984 with the induction of A. B. Carlson, Elmer and Esther Franks, Ture Johnson, Anson and Ella Rhodes, Will and Rena Richards, and Cliff Rossiter. In 1985, Glenn and Elsie DeGroft, Otto F. and Emmy Hering, Paul McNish, Howard Messenger, Leland Schuler, and Howard Taylor were honored. Howard McNish, N. C. and Mabel Patterson, Paul and Clara Jean Richards, and Kenneth and Dorothea Sperry were inducted in the ceremonies of 1986. The recipients of the awards for 1987 were Paul Adams, George and Catharine Binnig, Ignatius Cavanagh, Dick and Ruth Timmons, and George and Clare Timmons. In 1988, Lynn H. Hosford and Thomas L. White were inducted.

On March 31, 1989, the Hall of Fame program was held at the Patterson Center to honor Ralph Grosvenor and Hilton Farley.
Courtesy of the Patterson Center

This is the perfect team of products that are strictly Geauga County. The mixes are packaged in heavy canvas bags to prolong the shelf life. Corn Pancake Mix and Griddle Cake Pancake Mix are priced at $3.49 for two pounds. An eight ounce bottle of syrup costs $5.00.
Courtesy of Richards Maple Products

This is a fifth grade student's conception of a story from The Journal of Emily Nash. The Nash Family moved to Troy Township in February 1813. Emily and John are eight and seven years old in the syrup making season of 1815. The spelling and punctuation are Emily's, but the story was written after she was an adult.

"... is trying to make some shugar he left the syrup in the kettle over sunday the oxen found it and drinked it all up and it bloated the best one so he was like to die   farther thought he could tap him near the hip bone where the panch is close to the hide so he did so and put a quill into the hole but he was so bloated so full and hard the quill would fly out it had to be held there we had got the frame barn done and tied the oxen up there someone had got to stand by the ox and hold the quill in to the hole to let the wind out it made a noise like a whistle whistle John and I staid to the barn all night we took turns about standing by the ox one sit on the manger and hold the lantern while the other held the quill about the time the roosters began to crow farther came to see how we were geting along the bloat had gone down considerable he told us we had been good children we could go to the house he would stand by the ox till morning and would make each of us a pair of shoes so we saved the ox and got some shoes to wear to meeting and to school"
Courtesy of Ryan Robinson

HERE TO THERE

CHAPTER 7

Considering that the settlement of Geauga County began from the center with Burton in 1798, most traveling was through dense forests. Often the closest services, such as mills, were at least twenty miles away. As expressed by Henry Howe in his *Historical Collections of Ohio* (written in 1888) regarding Geauga County: "The difficulties of procuring subsistence for a family, in such circumstances, must be obvious. Often would a man leave his family in the wilderness with a stinted supply of food, and with his team or pack-horse go perhaps some twenty or thirty miles for provisions. The necessary appendages of his journey would be an axe, a pocket compass, fireworks, and blanket and bells. He cut and beat his way through the woods with his axe, and forded almost impassable streams."

The *Pioneer and General History of Geauga County*, 1953, describes early transportation in this way:

"Because of the high terrain, transportation development was retarded in Geauga County. Water courses accommodated many settlers. Some pioneers entered the region over one of the oldest routes in Ohio, the 'Girdled Road,' the first thoroughfare in the Western Reserve. Beginning at the western boundary of Pennsylvania, it entered the Reserve in southeast Trumbull County and passed through the northern part of Middlefield, slightly east of Chardon. Its name was derived from the girdled trees which marked the route. The next highway through the county passed through the western tier of townships. It was the old 'Chillicothe Road,' laid out by the territorial government. Capt. Edward Paine, of Chardon, was one of the committee which planned the route. A post road, established by the federal government in 1825, ran from Parkman to the towns

These men certainly do not have an enviable job, as they are surveying for the railroad to go through Middlefield. This photo was taken about 1870. One can imagine the obstacles outside of the weather that this crew encountered, considering the terrain between Chardon and Middlefield alone.
Courtesy of Shetler Printing/Roose Drug

of Windsor and Mesopotamia in Trumbull County."

Chillicothe Road, which was surveyed in 1801, became State Route 306. Other major north to south roads in the county include: Auburn Road going through Auburn Center, Newbury, and north to Painesville; State Route 44 (Painesville-Ravenna Road) which passes through Chardon, misses Burton by three miles to the west, and then through Auburn Corners; and State Route 528 (Madison Road) which goes through Parkman, misses Middlefield to the east by one mile, and through Thompson to Lake County. Route 700 starts at Burton and moves south through Welshfield to Portage County. State Routes 608 (Old State Road), 168, and 86 travel from northwest to southeast in the county. The major east to west routes are (from north to south): Federal Route 6 (Grand Army of the Republic (G.A.R.) Highway); State Route 322 (Mayfield Road); State Route 87 (Kinsman Rd.); and State Route 422. There are no major interstate highways passing through Geauga County, but Federal Route 6 can be traveled coast to coast.

In 1989 the responsibility for maintenance of state routes, including paving, patching, and snow removal, rests with the Ohio State Department of Transportation. In 1986 and 1987 major renovation and additional facilities were constructed at the State Highway garage in Burton. Burton's central location in the county promotes easy access for the state crews. Generally speaking, the county engineer, who in 1989 is Robert L. Phillips, is responsible for the maintenance of those roads which pass through multiple townships. Townships and villages maintain their self-contained streets and roads as approved by their trustees and councils respectively.

RAILROADS

One of the most controversial issues which faced the fledgling Western Reserve was the development of a convenient system of transportation to the South. With rivers coming into Lake Erie at Cleveland (Cuyahoga), Painesville (Grand), and Ashtabula (Conneaut), the major initial competition was for a canal to reach to the Ohio River. Politics were played to the hilt with many hard feelings occurring when Cleveland got the nod. At that time Cleveland was not the leader in population. Painesville with Geauga County on its side had that distinction. It was decided that a canal through Lake and Geauga Counties would be impractical. Then the railroads came along to offer the perfect alternative. Railroad transportation began in Geauga County in 1856 when the Painesville and Hudson Company completed its line. The Painesville & Youngstown Railroad, and the Geauga, Cleveland & Mahoning Valley Railway completed their respective lines in 1872 and 1874. In 1953, there were three railroad companies maintaining their service in the county. They were the Baltimore & Ohio, the Erie, and the Wheeling & Lake Erie. The 1980s saw the end of railroad service in Geauga County when the Baltimore and Ohio stopped its service and tore out the tracks. The right-of-way for that railroad is still evident, and work has been in progress to establish a bicycle trail along that road.

The interurban electric traction lines came into Geauga County in the 1890s. They provided a great service to the people of the county with public transportation to most areas of the county and to Cleveland. Because of the roads in the county being paved and the increasing numbers of automobiles, the Cleveland & Eastern Railway discontinued service in 1925. Today, with increased petroleum prices, threat of shortages, increasing costs of buying and maintaining automobiles, many people bemoan the loss of public transportation. Certainly cost of road paving and maintenance to accommodate personal vehicles add to the attractiveness of such a proposition, but I know very few who would give up their freedom to get up and go at will in their classy cars. But, another option would be nice.

AIRPORTS

In 1929, an airport was built in Parkman lying north of the town between State Routes 528 and 168 near State Route 88. It only lasted for ten years, and the operation was moved to Champion, Ohio. In the fifties Walter Best had an original airport hangar which Cleveland Hopkins moved to the hill above the Best Sand operations on Ravenna Road south of Chardon. The hangar is still there but no longer used as a hangar. The airfield and runway are still being used by the Cleveland Soaring Society (gliders) in 1989.

In 1964 Ohio Governor James A. Rhodes began a County Airport Development Program with a goal that every county in the state would have an airport to promote business development. As part of that program the Geauga County Airport was built in Middlefield in 1965. Through state, county, and Middlefield community financial and moral support, the airport was dedicated on September 29, 1968, with Governor Rhodes flying in for the ceremonies. The airport was operated by Geauga Air Services and Falcon Aviation until 1975, when Firebird Aviation took over the responsibilities. The Geauga County commissioners own the runway and land, while Firebird owns the buildings and equipment.

In spite of the natural obstacles present in Geauga County, there has been a tremendous amount of progress made in the transportation systems. It has taken and continues to take much hard work and planning to keep up with the times.

This old stone-arched bridge spans the East Branch of the Chagrin River which flows under Fowlers Mill Road in Munson Township. The bridge was built by Michael Flahaven of Thompson who learned the trade of stone mason in his native Ireland. It was considered to be an unusually fine example of stone work when it was built about 1870.

The bridge replaced a wooden structure which had collapsed, letting a team and wagon drop into the creek below. Photograph by Jim Warren and Sons, Action Photographers; courtesy of Jane Bushman

"Mud! Mud! Oh, this mud! are the first words that greet our ears when we meet a neighbor now a days, and from present prospects it seems a likely cry for months to come." Such was the news from Auburn in January of 1880 as reported in the Geauga Republican. The news was probably no different in Middlefield where this photograph was taken. One set of car tracks disappear to the north on State Route 608. If the photograph was taken in 1989 the photographer would be standing in the street between the Middlefield Municipal Center and the former White Brothers' Plaza. The roads in that area were not paved until between 1908 and 1917.
Courtesy of Shetler Printing/Roose Drug

Trains played an extremely important role in the development of industry in Geauga County. This B&O (Baltimore & Ohio) train was just about to cross Main Street in Middlefield at the turn of the century. The B&O ran from Fairport Harbor carrying coal and iron ore to Pittsburgh. Courtesy of Shetler Printing/Roose Drug

The Chagrin Falls line of the interurban ran through Newbury with a station in South Newbury at the intersection of Bell Road and State Route 44. Noting the conditions of the roads in the picture, one can certainly see the appeal of utilizing the traction system in the early twentieth century.
Courtesy of Anderson Allyn

The interurban turns the corner on to High Street in front of the Bell Vernon Creamery in Middlefield. Middlefield was fortunate in that there were two interurban lines coming into the village, a branch of the Cleveland-Chardon line through Burton and a line from Chagrin Falls. Groups could charter a streetcar to go to the theatre, a baseball game, or other special event in Cleveland. Two hours and fifteen minutes was thought to be a good time in which to get to Cleveland. The lines were developed in the 1890s and discontinued in 1925. The paving of the roads and the development of affordable cars spelled the end to an important era of Geauga County growth. Courtesy of Shetler Printing/Roose Drug

On February 22, 1900, the Cleveland & Eastern Railway carried its first passengers on the Burton and Middlefield line. This station in Burton was located at the Fairgrounds at the bottom of the Burton hill on the north side of the fair entrance road. After interurban service ceased in 1925, the garage portion of this building was eliminated. The remaining portion of the building was turned around and still serves as the offices for the Fair Board. Courtesy of Shetler Printing/Roose Drug

Paving of Middlefield Streets began around 1915. The cement mixer can be seen in the distance in this view of East Elm Street (later East High Street) from Main Street (State Route 608). Note the street light over the intersection. Courtesy of Shetler Printing/Roose Drug

Parkman Band members look solemn on arrival at the old Cleveland and Eastern Station in Burton. The Buckeye Band was formed in 1886 and well known throughout northern Ohio. The group celebrated its 50th anniversary in 1936, and at that time still had thirty members. Courtesy of Shetler Printing/Roose Drug

Today we take earth-moving equipment and tractors for granted, especially in light of utilizing horse, mule, and oxen-drawn equipment to achieve the same purposes. The road being straightened here is Hosford Hill north of Chardon on what is now Ravenna Road.
Courtesy of Stanlae Merritt

The truck in this photograph is loaded with gravel and being turned on a turntable. This took place on May 5, 1928, on State Route 322 at Fowlers Mill in Munson Township.
Courtesy of Shetler Printing/Roose Drug

The A. J. Ronyak Paving Company and the Geauga County Highway Department work together to resurface a stretch of Auburn Road south from Mentor Road to Route 6 at a cost of nearly forty five thousand dollars in June 1980. Deputy Engineer John Swift (on crutches) watches as pavers approach a hill crest section.
Photograph by Doris Cook, courtesy of the Geauga Times Leader

The Geauga County Airport held its Fourth Annual Air Show in 1982 to benefit the Multiple Sclerosis Society. Pilots Paul Grieshaber, left, and Bob Anspach check out an SNJ-4 Navy aircraft carrier trainer which was featured in the show. Photograph by Marie MacMurray, courtesy of the Geauga Times Leader

Geauga Transit began in 1976–1977 to provide public transportation within Geauga County with a priority of service to the elderly and handicapped of the county. Though not a taxi service, Geauga Transit can provide for any resident who does not have a means of transportation. The service is provided on a first come, first served basis with three to five days lead time needed for route planning and timing. In 1989 this service, which receives federal, state, and county monies, maintains ten vehicles. Fees are based on mileage required, and they are: 0 to 10 miles—$1.00; 11 to 20 miles—$1.50; 20 to 30 miles—$2.00. Half fares are charged to the elderly (over sixty-five years old) and handicapped riders. The director of Geauga Transit in 1989 is Jeff Nokes, and the operations manager is Steve Wells.

Friday is THE shopping day for the Amish community as shown here in a view north from the rear of Roose Drug store. Note that the parking accommodates both cars and buggies.
Courtesy of Shetler Printing/Roose Drug

125

GETTING DOWN TO BUSINESS

This view of Main Street in Chardon at the turn of the century indicates that the twentieth century began on a prosperous note. Besides automobiles instead of horses the most significant outside change in this picture is the Chardon House Hotel sitting at the south end of the street. Norman Canfield began a hotel on that location in 1812. With the log cabin being outgrown by demand, a frame hotel was built in 1818. D. W. Stocking bought the hotel in the late 1830s from Judge B. F. Avery, and added a third floor, complete with a ballroom to accommodate over three hundred people. The hotel changed hands a couple of times before a fire in March 1879. The owners were going to build a smaller hotel, but Judge H. K. Smith with other citizens raised two thousand dollars to restore the original size. Rebuilding by George Brakeman began in June and the formal reopening was in October. In 1912 S. D. Hollenbeck bought the hotel, did extensive remodeling, and renamed it the Highland Hotel. In 1937, L. M. Smith purchased the hotel, and soon after it was razed. There was also a hotel on the north end built in 1871. It was successively called the "Burnett House," "Geauga House," back to Burnett, "Bower House," "Park House," "Park Hotel," and in 1915 S. D. Hollenbeck, who at the time also owned the Highland Hotel, purchased the building. He remodeled it, and it became the Hollenbeck Apartments. The Bank One Building is on that site in 1989.

CHAPTER 8

EARLY INDUSTRY

As with most new areas to be settled, business in Geauga County started for survival. Early pioneers worked at surviving. As communities developed people began to do the skills that they brought with them. In Geauga County, most of those skills had to do with agriculture, so most business and industry spawned from the needs of an agricultural community. General stores brought in things that the community itself could not produce, and also provided a place for individual skills to be marketed.

The mills were an example of businesses providing services to the community. The streams in the county provided the power for gristmills and sawmills, and later for more sophisticated factories.

When it was possible to market beyond the community, the strength of the community began to grow. Because of a better route to the Southern states through Ohio and the Ohio River, Geauga County was able to corner the market on cheese in the 1830s. Producers in Auburn and Bainbridge were able to pool their efforts, learn from successful cheese factories in New York, and provide a quality product for another area of the country.

With the cheese factories grew the box factories to supply cheese boxes. With the timber being such a valuable resource, basket factories also grew. Timber resources are still being utilized in Geauga County. In 1986, through a survey done by the Geauga County Planning Commission, it was found that there were over a dozen major companies dealing with wood related products, and the Amish operations were not represented. Pallets, fences, and raw hardwood processing and distribution made up the majority of those enterprises.

Natural resources found in the county, in general, formed the backbone of industry. Stone quarries were found and developed in Thompson and Chardon. The fairly high iron content in the soil combined with the silica made brickmaking a feasible enterprise in many areas of the county. Maple syrup and apple cider made more use of the timber. The

127

combination of fresh water springs and grain production brought several distilleries into the area, such as the one Lemuel Punderson had at one end of his lake.

COMMERCE

Every township had its general store, and as the county prospered, more diverse establishments took root. Again, most of them were service operations to support the community, such as blacksmiths and cobblers. Because of the stables in the county in 1989 and the needs of the Amish community, there are still blacksmiths in Geauga County.

Hundreds of stores have come and gone in the county's history. Sometimes they passed with the passing of their owners. Sometimes they failed because of hard economic times. There were those who failed because they didn't do good business.

In more recent times, some regional commercial patterns had adverse effects on business in Geauga County. In the 1960s, shopping malls began to take over the shopping centers of the 1950s. Geauga County had fared pretty well in the shopping center era with developments like the Chardon Plaza and the Chesterland Shopping Center. But, when the Great Lakes Mall was built in Mentor, Ohio, in Lake County, it seemed that most retailers in Geauga County took it on the chin. It wasn't a problem for Geauga County residents to get into their cars and travel for as much as forty-five minutes to "go to the mall."

Fortunately, many persisted, and it seems that more and more people are finding that smaller centers and individually owned stores are a more pleasant way to shop. The county fought back also with centers of their own, such as the Tanglewood Mall in Bainbridge, the Harrington Square Mall in Middlefield, and Big Wheel Plaza made their way in the 1970s. Now, in the 1980s, the smaller shopping centers are coming back. Commercial building is taking place at a rapid pace in Chesterland, Bainbridge, and Chardon especially. Additionally, cottage industries have returned to popularity, and many signs in front of homes promoting services and businesses within can be seen when traveling throughout the county. Many people are finding quality products and services right around the corner. It sounds almost like the way things got started.

INDUSTRY

As mentioned before, most industry in Geauga County's beginnings was related to agriculture. As transportation systems became more efficient, especially the trains, Geauga County began to expand into other dimensions. The industry that has probably done the most to put Geauga County, Ohio, on the world map is rubber processing. Even through the hard times, this industry has stayed in the forefront of developing clean industry in the county. The success stories of Johnson Rubber, Chardon Rubber, Burton Rubber Processing, and other smaller operations have caused other industries to look on Geauga County as a favorable place from which to do business.

The county has been blessed with many innovators in diverse industrial and service areas, and a sampling of these are included in the photographs. Again, we could devote an entire book to Geauga County's present industries, let alone the past. Geauga County is one of the highest per capita income counties in Ohio, and that has not been a mistake. Geauga County in 1989 has one of the lowest unemployment percentages in the state. Another part of the reason for high per capita income in the county is the increasing numbers of people who work in Cuyahoga County and have found that Geauga County is a nicer place to live. But that by no means diminishes the strides that have taken place in industry in Geauga County. Geauga residents can take great pride in the products and services that come from their county.

This is a photo of the Newbury Box Factory. "G. W. Stafford came from Auburn to Newbury in the early 1890s and purchased the sawmill, west of the (Newbury) Center, from Neaves and Hodges. He employed 18 men, and the manufacture of cheese boxes was one of its projects; the men turned out between 700 and 800 each day. These were sold and delivered on wagons with big racks and drawn by horses. About 300 boxes were considered a load ... The mill burned in 1902, but was immediately rebuilt and fitted up with modern machinery, and continued to operate until the time of Mr. Stafford's death." (text from Pioneer and General History of Geauga County, *1953, page 651)*

The first hotel in Troy was opened in 1842, in the home of J. E. Sperry with A. J. Nash as landlord. Soon after its opening the hotel was moved to its present site where the Welshfield Inn now stands. A front porch has been added to the original building. The beams of the original building add old country charm to the restaurant, which is still popular in 1989.
Courtesy of Shetler Printing/Roose Drug

In 1894–1895, Charles Alexander built a basket factory in the southeast corner of Montville Township. It employed thirty to forty workers and, after five or six years, it was converted to a sawmill and veneer factory. The date on the photograph was May 27, 1911. Alexander also put up a store and obtained a post office named Damon. All of these were on the "Old Plank Road" (State Route 86). After the sawyer, Bill Barnes, was killed by the breaking of the saw, the operations stopped, and the sawmill burned. The area was abandoned.
Courtesy of Shetler Printing/Roose Drug

Neher and Mills became the Scotland General Store and is still in business in 1989. It is on the south side of Route 322 just east of Caves Road in Chesterland.
Couretsy of Sylvia Wiggins

The Bruce Brothers bought this store from Lucretia Taylor in 1887. They added an undertaking business to the general store. Willard bought out his brother's share and in 1937 celebrated fifty years of storekeeping. Mr. Bruce died a month later, but Mrs. Bruce and her brother, Ward Thompson, continued to run the store. In 1943 it was sold to Otto Van Orsdale.
Courtesy of Shetler Printing/Roose Drug

Since 1943 the store on the northwest corner of Claridon Center (intersection of Claridon-Troy Road and Mayfield Road) has had many owners and served a variety of purposes including a gift shop, later a balloon shop. In 1989 it has become Claridon Antiques, and the store looks better than ever.

This photo of the Ohio Pail Company sparks one of the greatest industrial success stories in Geauga County. In 1895, Joe Johnson talked Howard and Walter Shellito into centralizing all their wooden pail manufacturing in Middlefield. Johnson soon joined their business whose name changed from Udall-Shellito Company to Ohio Pail Company in 1914. Around 1920 wooden pails gave way to steel pails. Johnson, who by then was company president, devised a flat, rubber tube to help seal the lid of paint, oil, and ink pails, and later set up the Johnson Rubber Company to keep up with the demand for gaskets. In 1936, the pail operations were sold, and the company became the Johnson Rubber Company. The Depression, increasing competition, and declining profits plagued the company until William F. Miller, an attorney from Toledo, helped bring the company around. After confidently investing his own money into the company, he became its president in 1946. Much growth occurred in the 1950s, including a Flooring Products Division. The 1960s found a market for a water-lubricated bearing used on marine vessel propeller shafts. In 1981 the parent company of Duramax, Inc., was formed to provide a broader base for the firm's continued expansion and diversification. Duramax Incorporated organizations encompass five operations outside of Middlefield in the United States and Canada. In 1989, the company's chairman of the board is William F. Miller's son, Paul C. Miller, Sr., and the president and chief executive officer is Paul C. Miller, Jr.
Courtesy of Shetler Printing/Roose Drug

This is the Montville store of T. J. Sealy who was the undertaker and proprietor of furniture and hardware sales. The lady on horseback is his daughter, Edith. A few years after this picture was taken in 1896, S. S. Welchman bought the property, and after his death his daughter Nellie took over. She ran the store until she retired in 1971.
Courtesy of Shetler Printing/Roose Drug

John Henry Morse of Huntsburg turns rags into carpeting on his loom. Other materials were made on the loom. He could take wool from a customer and return it to them in a suit or dress. The wool was carded in a mill in Thompson, but Morse did the spinning and weaving.

Morse was born in Huntsburg in 1840 and died in 1918. He had already been making clothes for the family when he was asked to make a wedding jacket for a neighbor. His first job for pay came when he was twelve years old.

His real talent, however, was in dressmaking. "When the ladies of the family dressed to go out in his creations they had to look 'just so.' If they didn't pass his inspection, he would mumble something about their inability to dress themselves and proceed to pull and tug at their gowns until they hung to suit him."

The Amish of Huntsburg and Middlefield always went to Morse to have him make the strange attire of their sect. He was working on an Amishman's suit and became too ill to finish it even with the help of his great-niece, Merribelle (Pickett) Young. The Amish man came and said he would get an Amish lady to finish it.
Photograph by Jim Warren, courtesy of Violet Warren

The Henry Thompson store was located on the south side of High Street in Middlefield just east of the intersection of Old State Road (State Route 608). Mr. Thompson, whose great-grandfather, Isaac Thompson was the first settler in Middlefield, was active in the Middlefield community for over fifty years. His widow, Eugenie, ran the store until 1943. Mrs. Thompson sold the store to Edith Ritchie, who sold the building in 1947.
Courtesy of Shetler Printing/Roose Drug

Thompson House was located north of the park in Thompson and on the east side of Route 528 in 1900. Maria Exceen and Eliza Clapp are standing on the porch. Eliza (?) Clapp Wright died in 1912 and is buried in Huntsburg. Marie Exceen died September 1, 1896 and is buried in Thompson.
Courtesy of the Geauga Oral History Project

The Chardon Macaroni Company was organized in 1902 and the factory was completed early in the next year. Macaroni was produced at a rate of twenty-five to forty barrels a day. In 1906, the factory was leased to the Youngstown Macaroni Company. After a year the factory burned, and they withdrew from the Chardon plant. It was then sold to the Cleveland Macaroni Company in 1907 and was known as the Pioneer Macaroni Company, only to be turned back to the Cleveland Company and known as a branch. Extensive improvements were made in 1910. The business thrived until the scarcity of flour due to World War I caused the factory to close. Through the years several different kinds of plants tried to utilize the factory, and in 1933 it was purchased by the Chardon Rubber Company.
Courtesy of the Geauga Republican

The First National Bank of Burton opened in 1902 with deposits of about $16,000. By 1948 deposits were at $3.25 million. The bank merged with the Huntington National Bank of Columbus in 1980. At the time of the merger the First National Bank of Burton had assets over $80 million and six branch offices located throughout Geauga County.
Courtesy of the Geauga Times Leader

"G. L. Chapman Boots, Shoes, Gent's Furnishings" is the caption under his picture in the 1900 Atlas of Geauga County. He became the sole owner of the business in 1900. When he retired in 1945 he had been in business exactly fifty years.

Bert Barnum worked at the store after school and Saturdays. He bought the business and retained the name. The ladder was manufactured by the Bicycle Step Ladder Company, Chicago (patented December 10, 1890).

When Bert retired, the business was purchased by Bob Majka. The name of the store hasn't changed, and the inside furnishings are still the same.
Photograph by Maude Beech, courtesy of the Geauga Oral History Project

Minterns Lunch and Ice Cream Stand was built circa 1927 in front of the Converse house on the north side of State Route 422 east of the State Route 528 intersection. Raymond "Buck" Dolezal, Parkman historian, recalled that in his youth he and his friends would go into Minterns and buy their pint of hand-packed ice cream for fifteen cents and sit on the front stone ledge of the store to listen for the cars coming down Rt. 422. The skill was determining what make of car was coming by the sounds it made before it came into sight. In 1940 the road was widened and the large elm trees in front were cut down. Minterns was remodeled around that time and became the Post House Restaurant which is still there today.
Courtesy of Shetler Printing/Roose Drug

C. E. Rickard opened his bakery in 1910, renting what had been Avery's Store next to the fire department on the square. In 1916, he purchased the present site of the store, which is on the street level of the I.O.O.F. building. He did not move the bakery to that location until 1920. Mr. Rickard retired in 1946 when his son, Lewis, had returned from World War II ready to take over the business. In the 1980s, the next generation has carried on with the bakery, as Lewis' son, Mark, and daughter, Robin, keep the business going. Since the beginning of the store, one of the most popular items has been the salt rising bread, a pungent, Yankee concoction. The pungency comes from the dough starter having to ferment.

The I.O.O.F. Hall and building, after years of deterioration, was restored and renovated by artist Dennis Killeen in 1987 and 1988. Mr. Killeen has brought back the elegance of the past in his work.

The Chardon Rubber Company was incorporated January 16, 1930, with R. L. Bostwick as president. The company began production in rented space on the south end of the building owned by Chardon Development Company on the west side of Washington Street between Fifth Avenue and Center Street. They were able to purchase the property on which the old Macaroni Factory had operated in 1933, and at once were able to double their work crew and production. Chardon Rubber obtains raw rubber from all over the world. The rubber is processed and cured with some being sold to other rubber companies and the rest kept for the manufacture of products within the plant. The extruded rubber products they make include gaskets, washers, hoses, molding, and all types of mechanical rubber articles. The company also maintains a plastics division for extruding tubing and hoses. Chardon Rubber products can be found all over the world and throughout the United States, especially in automobiles and appliances. One of the plastic extrusion machines runs twenty-four hours a day, seven days a week making hoses for use inside washing machines. In 1989, the chief executive officer for Chardon Rubber Company is Jefferson W. Keener, Jr. The company employs over 650 people and has been especially supportive of the Chardon Public Schools.

Anderson Allyn, Sr., started Chardon Metal Products Company in 1945. The company has produced steel, aluminum, copper, stainless and brass fabricated tubing products for a wide variety of industrial and military uses, including hydraulic lines and oil return lines; residential and industrial plumbing; and automotive aftermarket applications. In addition, the company has produced precision screw machine parts for manufacturers of automotive replacement products, industrial components, small tools, and appliances. In 1955, Chardon Metal Products moved to its present location on Fifth Avenue in Chardon, leading the way for industrial development in that area. Mr. Allyn has been instrumental in promoting the development of locally owned banking. His initial involvement was with Geauga County National Bank. In the 1980s, he turned his attention to the development of the First County Bank in Chardon. Mr. Allyn has also been very active in the Chardon Area Chamber of Commerce and the Pilgrim Christian Church in Chardon. In 1980, he turned the reins of Chardon Metal Products over to his son, Anderson "Spike" Allyn, Jr., although Mr. Allyn, Sr. remains as chairman of the board in 1989.
Photograph by Jim Anderson

Stock Equipment Company is an engineering company which designs and manufactures coal-handling equipment for industrial and commercial power plants, radwaste equipment for nuclear power plants, incineration systems, and special products. Arthur J. Stock founded the company as Stock Engineering Company in 1929 to design special machinery and develop new products for the utility industry. The first product, the CONICAL nonsegregating coal distributor, was invented and developed by Arthur Stock and is still being manufactured today. Product manufacturing was moved from Cleveland, Ohio, into what had been the village blacksmith shop owned by Horace Shippey in Bainbridge Township. In 1943 the company acquired eleven acres of land at its present site on Chillicothe Road (State Route 306) north of State Route 422. The company was incorporated in 1950 and the name changed to Stock Equipment Company. In December, 1980, Stock became a division of General Signal Corporation of Stamford, Connecticut. In 1989, the chief executive officer is Joseph K. Tannehill. The company employs approximately three hundred people with 147,000 square feet of buildings.
Courtesy of Stock Equipment Company

R. W. Sidley, Incorporated, was founded in 1933 by Robert W. Sidley in Thompson, Geauga County, Ohio and incorporated in 1938. Silica mining operations began in the early thirties in Thompson. In 1946 Mr. Sidley entered the ready-mix concrete business and in 1948 purchased the Thompson Silica Company which is located on State Route 528 just south of Thompson. The company added to its Geauga County operations in 1961 with a ready-mix batch plant and building supply operation on State Route 87 in Newbury. The photo is of the Newbury facility. Robert W. Sidley passed away in 1961 at the age of fifty-five and was succeeded by his son, Robert C. Sidley, who is the present Chief Executive Officer. In 1962 the company expanded into the precast concrete industry, and that plant is also located in Thompson. The company has expanded to be able to supply construction materials to five Northeastern Ohio counties including Geauga, Lake, Ashtabula, Trumbull, and Mahoning.

White Brothers Super Market began as a small fruit business in the basement of the Knights of Pythias Hall facing Main Street (State Route 608) in 1946. The brothers were: Graydon, Ralph, Virgil, Lawrence, Lloyd, and Basil, the sons of Graydon White, Sr., and grandsons of Will White. The supermarket opened in 1947.
Courtesy of Shetler Printing/Roose Drug

Middlefield Electric Company had moved from its original location on the west side of South Main Street in Middlefield to this site on East High Street in the 1950s. Mr. and Mrs. Marten Merryfield, Sr., came from Orwell, Ohio, in 1933. Mr. Merryfield worked as a rural mail carrier, and did some radio and electronic work in his off hours. Mrs. Merryfield opened the retail store next to the Mu-Mac Theatre. During World War II, the store sold paint because electrical supplies, especially copper, went to the war effort. In the late 1950s the Middlefield Electric building pictured became the Post Office, rented from the Merryfield family. Mr. Merryfield, Sr., retired in 1955, but the business was perpetuated by his son, Marten, Jr., and daughter-in-law, Hope. The electric business for a time shared the building where Dr. Albert Evans' office is located, on the other side of High Street. Then it moved to the Merryfield residence, where it stayed until 1977 when a new Merryfield Electric operation was built and opened on State Route 528, north of State Route 87. The Merryfield family, both generations, have been very active in the community.
Courtesy of Shetler Printing/Roose Drug

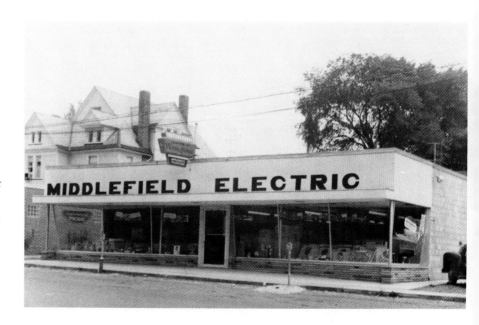

Jackson Lumber was established in Newbury in 1946 by Donald C. "Mike" Jackson and his wife, Francis. From the initial function of providing logs to basket factories and sawmills, Jackson has added a stationary sawmill, a millwork plant, and a dry kiln to create a diversified product line. The company now provides flooring, paneling, pallets and skids, and hardwood fences. Today Jackson Hardwood Lumber is operated by the Jackson sons, Ed and Art. Their operation is located on Music Street in Newbury.

Production began at Geauga Industries in 1947. In 1946, Adrian Welsh and Don Young resigned their positions at Johnson Rubber Company and incorporated this company for the manufacture of extruded rubber and plastics. The company was located just outside the village limits on South Main Street. In 1989, Geauga Industries is part of Carlisle Corporation, but it still specializes in custom rubber parts. The business employs three hundred workers and maintains 230,000 square feet of buildings for its operation. Courtesy of Shetler Printing/Roose Drug

In 1956 the Ohio regulations for milk production and distribution changed, and the greatest impact in Geauga County was on the Amish community. They needed an outlet for their milk, and Hans R. Rothenbuhler, a master cheesemaker, raised in the Emmenthaler Valley near Berne, Switzerland, came to Geauga County with the solution. Hence, the Middlefield Swiss Cheese Co-op was formed, and the first cheese was produced on July 4, 1956. From that initial two hundred pounds of cheese, the Middlefield Cheese House has progressed to a yearly production of approximately twenty million pounds of Middlefield Swiss Cheese. That's over ten thousand tons! The Cheese House now has a store with many imported food items, and it houses a modern museum which chronicles the Middlefield story and the Swiss heritage behind the cheese. Hans Rothenbuhler died in 1984 of injuries sustained in a skiing accident, a tragic loss for his family and the Middlefield community. His family maintains the management of the business.

The American Society for Metals came to Geauga County in 1959. Metals Park is located in Novelty on Kinsman Road (State Route 87). The unique tri-level building built into the hillside sits under the geodesic dome designed by R. Buckminster Fuller. The dome stands 103 feet high, 274 feet in diameter at its base, and weighs eighty tons. It is constructed of a network of hexagonal and pentagonal shapes formed of thirteen miles (65,000 parts) of aluminum tubing and rods in tension. The dome is mounted on five pylons, the foundations of which reach 77 feet beneath the earth's surface. The dome is the largest of its kind in the world.
Courtesy of the Geauga Times Leader

Newbury Industries was founded in 1955 and incorporated in 1957 for the purpose of producing laboratory type injection molding machinery for use by schools, laboratories, and model shops. It came about through the uniting of the R. L. Frohring Machine Company founded in 1942, and the Glenn Machine and Service Corporation. Basically, the Frohring operation provided the custom machine shop, and the Glenn operation provided custom machine design expertise. Typical products produced on Newbury equipment are bottle caps, combs, sunglasses, molded electric cord sets and connectors, gears, tableware, and components for the electronic, automotive, and appliance industry. Newbury Industries has done pioneering work in the field of screw plasticizing, two color molding, rubber and thermoset molding, plus producing design equipment for integration into automatic production lines. The company is located on Kinsman Road (State Route 87) just west of Auburn Road.

Hambden Building Products was started in 1959 by George Zakany, a contractor who had moved from Cleveland to Geauga County in 1950. Mr. Zakany bought an L-shaped piece of land in Hambden off the corner of State Route 608 and Federal Route 6. Eventually Mr. Zakany gave the land accessing Route 6 to the Hambden Congregational Church which was located on the northeast corner of the intersection, and he gave the back acreage of the property with access to Route 6 to Hambden Township for a new township park. Mr. Zakany died in 1988, but he left a legacy with his generosity and his workmanship. He owned Hambden Building Products along with Lydia Newell, and his son-in-law, Mike Chapman, and they continue to maintain the business. Ray Chapman, Mike's brother is the store manager.

This authentic medicine wagon is a fixture in the Swiss Cheese Festival parades in Middlefield. Rick Roose of Roose Drug Store not only promotes the heritage of the days gone by with this wagon, but his store is decorated with much memorabilia from apothecary shops and pharmacies. His attention to the history of the community has spawned a great file of historical photographs of Geauga County. That collection has proved to be an important part of this book, and Rick's help along with Garland Shetler's is greatly appreciated.
Courtesy of Shetler Printing/Roose Drug

Kinetico founded in 1970, has grown from a two-man operation into an organization that employs more than 160 people. Founded by Bill Prior, president (right), and Jim Kewley, vice president, Kinetico has become a major force in the water processing industry. The photograph is of the goundbreaking for their second building which took place on December 29, 1982. Kinetico manufactures water processing equipment that is geared to rural and urban residential applications as well as commercial and industrial applications. Looking to solve special problems Kinetico has developed and now produces custom designed softening, deionization, and metals recovery systems for industry, hospitals, and laboratories. The Engineered Systems Division has also made great strides in developing unique processes that recirculate toxic materials, rather than pollute existing water supplies. The company is also developing a total water treatment system for homes served by municipal water. It is called "Waterplant." Kinetico is a prime example of a clean, innovative industry which has come into Geauga County, providing employment, supporting the schools, and also, with its beautiful grounds and facilities, keeping the county a lovely place to live.
Courtesy of the Geauga Times Leader

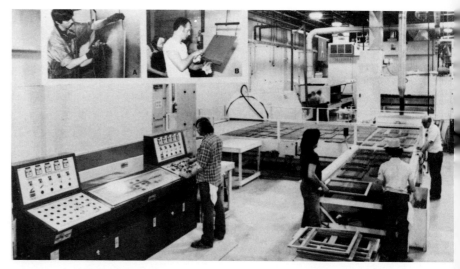

One of the real success stories of manufacturing in Geauga County is KraftMaid Cabinetry in Middlefield. Richard M. Moodie is the founder and president. KraftMaid, which began in 1969 in a suburban garage workshop, moved to Middlefield in 1984 to a 124,000-square-foot facility. Needing to expand even more the company will be moving into an even larger facility in 1989. Employing approximately 230 people, much of the quality control, and many operations are computerized. An oil based wiping stain is applied (A) and then hand wiped (B) to bring out the depth of grain. Any assortment of parts may be loaded (C) according to the production schedule.
Courtesy of KraftMaid Cabinetry, Inc.

The business community in Geauga County has always been in the forefront of support for the schools and education in the county. In this photo we see George White (on the right) of White Brothers presenting a check to Michael Ucchino (on the left), Cardinal High School principal, to pay for Resusa Annie, the lifelike model who is used in the teaching of CPR (cardio-pulmonary resuscitation) classes for the school and the community. Looking on is Ray Miller, a health teacher for Cardinal and a certified CPR instructor. This presentation took place in October of 1979.
Photograph by Doris Cook, courtesy of the Geauga Times Leader

Indicative of the commercial growth which continues to take place in Geauga County is the Teague Shopping Center in Newbury. Built in 1979, the shopping center in 1989 includes Newbury Pharmacy, Prots Food Center, Newbury Auto Parts, Geauga Savings Bank, Moster's Hardware, and Solon Cleaners.

Although built in 1988, the Washington Post Center in Chardon at the corner of Washington and Center Streets reflects the heritage of the area in its architecture. The Center is the home of Chardon Clothing Company, Village Booksellers, Sound Effects, and Geauga County Coins & Jewelry.

The Geauga Livestock Commission, located on Nauvoo Road north of Middlefield Village, is a busy place on Monday when Amish and Yankees bring their stock to sell or trade.
Photograph by Perry Cragg; courtesy of Doris Cragg

143

LEISURE—A CIVILIZER OF MAN

Mineral Lake Park in Middlefield has long been a source of recreation for the community. Located just south of the business district on the south side of Sperry Lane, it runs most of the length of that street between Old State Road and Lake Avenue. The park contains a shaded picnic area, tennis courts, and two baseball diamonds as well as Mineral Lake.
Courtesy of Shetler Printing/Roose Drug

CHAPTER 9

The title of this chapter is taken from a quote by Benjamin Disraeli. In an address on April 3, 1872, he stated, "Increased means and increased leisure are the two civilizers of man." Anyone who has experienced the stress of job or family, or had periods of poverty or no fun, can certainly agree that it is harder to be civilized. Thankfully, the times, occasions, and places exist in Geauga County to become more civilized.

PARADES AND CELEBRATIONS

Geauga County people have always found reasons to celebrate. Parades, reunions, community and school homecomings, centennials of towns and the county, bicentennials of our country and of its Constitution are just a few examples. There are the Maple Festival in Chardon, the Pumpkin Festival in Huntsburg, the Swiss Cheese Festival in Middlefield, the Apple Butter and Raccoon County Music Festivals in Burton and the Great Geauga County Fair. All of these yearly events draw not only residents from Geauga County, but people throughout the United States know that Geauga Countians know how to celebrate right. They come in thousands from counties, near and far, to celebrate with us. People, who have moved away, come back to touch base and share in the fun.

The histories of the county indicate that this phenomenon is not recent. The Geauga County Historical Society got its start from a family reunion. On July 24, 1873, 172 descendants of John and Easter Ford held their reunion at the old homestead in Burton. Initiated by Colonel Henry Hine Ford, others attending were Homer Goodwin, Judge Lester Taylor, and General James A. Garfield. Those people set into motion a means of celebrating the heritage of Geauga County.

PICNIC GROUNDS

There are times that families and friends need to go somewhere else for outdoor fellowship, and

145

Geauga County has many places where this can happen. The Geauga Park District, Punderson State Park, Pioneer Waterland, the township parks, private parks and farms have provided wonderful picnic areas.

HUNTING AND FISHING

There are two Ohio State designated hunting areas in Geauga County. They are Hambden Orchard on State Route 608 north of Sisson Road, and the Auburn Hunting Area on Auburn Road between Bell Road and State Route 422. Many farmers and land owners open their properties to responsible hunters, for often small game populations can get out of hand. The increasing whitetail deer population has brought about excellent deer hunting in the county.

There are great fishing areas in Geauga County. Punderson Lake is known for panfish and trout (stocked yearly). Lake Aquilla yields bass, northern pike, and panfish. LaDue Reservoir has given trophy bass, walleye, northern pike, and crappie to worthy fishermen. East Branch has similarly yielded bass, pike and crappie. The Geauga Park District ponds and lakes are excellent places to take children for panfishing. The rivers have a wide variety of fish and also provide beautiful canoe trips for even the novice canoeists.

CAMPGROUNDS

Punderson State Park provides a wide variety of public camping opportunities from tenting to cabins. There are also privately owned campgrounds throughout the county which furnish clean, modern facilities and activities.

GOLF COURSES

Golfers in Geauga County have many opportunities to test their skills. Included in the list are Auburn Springs Golf Course, Berkshire Hills Country Club, Fowler's Mill Golf Course, Pleasant Hill Golf Course, Punderson State Park, St. Denis, Orchard Hills Golf and Country Club, Hidden Valley Golf Course, Chardon Lakes Golf, Rolling Green Golf Club, and Grandview Inn and Golf Club. Private courses are Tanglewood Country Club and Legend Lake Golf Club.

CAMPS

Rural Geauga County provides great locations for camps for youth and adults. Camp Ho-Mita-Koda in Newbury provides an educational and recreational experience for diabetic children. Highbrook Lodge is a camp for the blind and visually handicapped. Other camps include Camp Burton, Camp Chickagami, Camp Wise and Camp Stigwandish.

AMUSEMENT PARKS

Geauga Lake is on the border of Geauga and Portage Counties. Hence, Geauga Lake Park and Sea World are close at hand for Geauga County residents. History states that people were picnicking at Giles Lake (now Geauga Lake) in the early 1800s.

Pioneer Waterland Park on Kile Road opened in 1984. The seventy-five acre water amusement park and campground contains six-story high waterslides, a lazy river inner tube ride, a three-acre activity pool, miniature golf, kiddie areas, picnic areas and other dry games on land.

BASEBALL, ETC.

There are baseball leagues for boys and girls of all ages throughout the county. Individual township and village recreation boards provide many activities for all ages throughout the year. The Geauga County YMCA continues to grow in its service to the community. The summer day camps are especially appreciated in the community. The "Y" has sponsored a church softball league and has been active in promoting soccer for the youth of the county.

Again, we speak of community as we recognize the value of leisure time and times of fun, and we are more civilized.

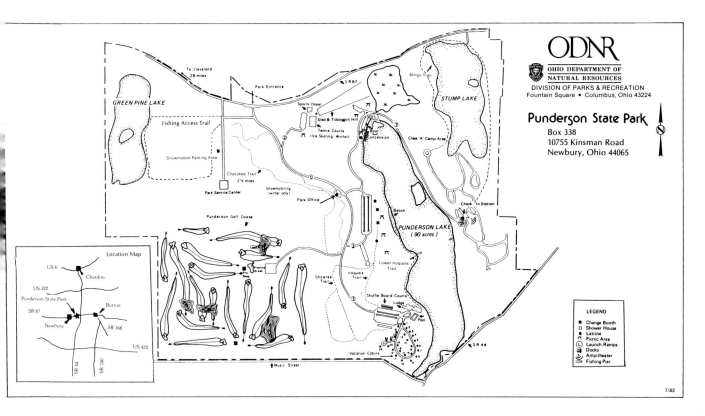

This map of Punderson State Park reflects the many possible activities at the park and indicates that it is a year-round activity center. The Manor House, cabins, and trailer and tent camping provide a variety of accommodations to suit every need. Fishing, tennis, golf, swimming, and hiking trails are some of the summer activities. A sled and toboggan hill, an ice-skating rink, snowmobile area, and cross country skiing highlight the winter possibilities.
Courtesy of Punderson State Park

The Manor House at Punderson State Park overlooks Punderson Lake which is one of several glacier lakes in northeast Ohio formed during the ice age. Lemuel Punderson came to the vicinity in 1808 from New Haven, Connecticut. He built his home, a gristmill and distillery near the foot of the lake. Mr. Punderson passed away in 1822 leaving 505 acres and the lake to his heirs who sold the property to W. B. Cleveland. Karl Long of Detroit purchased the property and planned to make it his summer home. Mr. Long started the construction of the mansion but after spending $250,000 was forced to abandon the project due to financial difficulties. The property reverted to W. B. Cleveland. The State of Ohio purchased the property in 1948, and when the Division of Parks was formed by a legislative act in 1949 the grounds became the responsibility of that Division. The Manor House was completely remodeled and opened to the public on November 15, 1956. Since that time, the Manor House has experienced a major structural renovation which began in 1979 and was finished in 1982.

The Newbury Cornet Band was organized in the early 1900s. Led by Ernest Finch and trained by Bliss Parkinson from Dana's Institute in Warren, the band played at many annual social events including the Burton Fair and the Chagrin Falls Fair. They performed in Cleveland on Labor Day in 1905, and played regularly at the bandstand in South Newbury near the chapel until State Route 44 was built and the stand had to be removed to make way.

Grant Nichols displays his catch of raccoons. His poolroom was located about where Huntington Bank is on the north side of Route 322, just west of Route 306. That area was known as Chester X (Cross) Roads. The township is Chester, but the post office is Chesterland.
Courtesy of Sylvia Wiggins

Chesterland Caves was a popular resort when the interurban operated. Passengers could disembark at the Pavilion which was between the Gates Mill and Scotland stops. Caves Road in Chester township acquired its name from the rocky formation.
Courtesy of Sylvia Wiggins

These two photos are scenes at the Wilson Smith stables which were located on the northwest corner where Park Avenue comes on to South Street in Chardon. Park Avenue was so called because of the horse race park at the bottom of the hill west of the Baltimore & Ohio Railroad tracks on the south side of the street. In the spring of 1888 the Chardon Driving Association was formed and commenced building a half-mile track under the direction of Wesley Goodrich. Also on the inside of the track was a baseball field. The track fell into disuse at the turn of the century because of a heavy spring rain, and the town and high school baseball teams played on the ball field only until 1908 when it was moved. Courtesy of Kim Glenn

One of the most clever fundraisers in county history was the Womanless Wedding. This occurred in 1920 in Chardon with the only female in the picture being Dorothy Parsons, the little flower girl in the middle of the picture.
Courtesy of Mrs. Dorothy Parsons Knapp

Highbrook Lodge on Aquilla Road in Claridon Township opened in 1928 as a summer camp for the blind and partially blind men and women. This building was constructed in 1956.

The camp is operated by the Cleveland Society for the Blind and is the oldest and longest running camp for the visually handicapped in the country. In 1958 it cost $30 to send one person to camp for eight days. In 1977, the cost for a week was $125.

Enjoying the warm weather of June 1980 at Highbrook Lodge for the visually handicapped are (from left to right): camp counselor Steve Carson, Robert Van Allen, counselor Nancy Schager, and Peter Casimatis. Marie, the Seeing Eye dog, is also happy to be outside.
Photograph by Neil Korey,
Courtesy of the Geauga Times Leader

Alpine Valley, located in Munson Township and taking advantage of being in Ohio's snow belt, opened in 1963. Three people who were instrumental in the success of the ski area are Skip Frank, Bill Harris, and Ferdl Aster. By 1983 the ski area had six lifts including a four-place chair lift sixteen hundred feet long. The chalet features a lounge, cafeteria, pizza shop, and seating capacity for over three hundred people in the main room. Several golf courses in Geauga County provide for cross-country skiing when the snow flies.
Courtesy of the Geauga Times Leader

The Czecho-Slovak people started to immigrate into this county in 1890. Taborville, an unincorporated community tucked away in the southwest corner of Auburn Township, is a Czechoslovakian enclave founded by immigrants in 1925. The community began as a gymnastics summer training center for Czech families in the Greater Cleveland Area. The initial Bohemian workmen bought two broken down farms, 136 total acres. In the space of eleven years, sixty-five cottages had been built, surrounded by gardens and orchards. This photograph depicts the Fourth of July celebration in 1930. In 1936 the first workers' Olympics was held in Taborville. Prominent guests included Dr. Frank Sowkeys, president of the Czech Senate. Ten thousand people saw one thousand gymnasts from all over the United States and Czechoslovakia perform. Activities for boys and girls are encouraged as there is a community house and dormitories for the boys' and girls' clubs.
Courtesy of the Geauga Times Leader

Dog sled Racing has become a favorite winter pastime and spectator event in Geauga County. In recent years, one of the frustrating aspects has been the mild weather occurring on the weekend planned for the big annual race.
Courtesy of the Geauga Times Leader

The Rug and Craft Show in Burton at the Century Village is an annual event which began in 1960. The show is usually held the weekend after Labor Day. Pictured right is Jim Anderson of Cottage Pottery in Burton demonstrating his craft during the 1979 event in which over eighty crafts people demonstrated their skills.
Courtesy of the Geauga Times Leader

Camp Chickagami is located on State Route 168 in Parkman. This Boy Scout Camp is owned by the Trumbull County Boy Scout Council and began as a camp in 1941. Natural water resources was one of the major factors which made the site a most favorable location. After the construction of a dam, a lake was formed, making it ideal for swimming and other water sports.

The Shangri La Ski Club in Parkman utilizes Moss Lake for water skiing in the summer months.

Most townships have a recreation park, either provided by the township trustees or part of the Geauga County Park District. Bill Pennell (holding the shovel) belonged to the Geauga Board of Realtors whose project in 1980 was the "Greening of America."

Helping with the work at Hambden Township Park are: Dawn Mack and Michael Bailey (standing), and Billy Bailey and Melissa Penell (kneeling).

The park has a pavilion, playground equipment, and ball diamonds suitable for various leagues.
Photograph by Sharon Haynes,
Courtesy of the Geauga Times Leader

Civil War re-enactments at the Burton Century Village are usually family affairs. This was the case in 1979 when the Warren family attended. They are (from left) Gary, Deborah, and father, Jim. The little papoose was from another tribe.

George Dauler of Chardon has performed a great service to the people of Geauga County with his one-man presentation of General U. S. Grant. He has brought history alive for many children and adults throughout Northern Ohio.
Photograph by Jill Coder-Sestak,
Courtesy of the Geauga Times Leader

The Beaux and Belles of Geauga County performed at the Geauga County Historical Society in June 1969. From left to right: David Booth, Bill "Lucky" Luckay, Lloyd Thomas, Ruth Booth (the organizer of the group during the 1950s), Kathleen "Kay" Cullum, Elizabeth "Lee" Fisher, Glenda Lehmann, and Ann DeMuth.

The group has had as many as twenty-five members; the current membership is nine. They have a lot of fun and provide good entertainment for group meetings, parades, and other festive occasions. Their performances are now limited to Geauga County.

One member not pictured is Gladys Vaughn who is the accompanist.
Courtesy of Geauga County Historical Society

Action has been heating up during the summer months at Thompson Drag Raceway since the 1950s. The raceway is located on Sidley Road in Thompson south of Rock Creek Road (State Route 166).
Courtesy of the Geauga Times Leader

A visitor to the Apple Butter Festival of October 1981 pretends to drive the Geauga Cannonball. The steam engine was brought to the festival by Frank Gillen of Newbury and used to give rides.

Steam engines are a collector's item, but some are still used on Amish farms.
Photograph by Doris Cook,
Courtesy of the Geauga Times Leader

*This aerial view of Middlefield shows the typical crowd at the annual Swiss Cheese Festival in early June.
Courtesy of the Shetler Printing/Roose Drug*

One of the more recent celebrations which has become an annual event in Geauga County is "Yesteryear in the Park." In this 1983 photograph is B. J. Shanower, the senior citizens' King for a Day, in his vintage car with Yesteryear Queen contestants (from left to right) Annette Gierlach, Sherry Ronyak, and Missy Lillibridge. The Yesteryear gala, including flower arranging, pie baking and cake decorating contests, Old Timers softball game, horse show, and parade has been held on the Fourth of July by the Friends of the Burton Library with proceeds going to support the library. Photograph by Doris Cook, Courtesy of the Geauga Times Leader

On the eighteenth green of Rolling Green Golf Club are (from left) Virgil Collier, Richard Wahl, who is the course manager, Fred Johnson and Andy Ule. The eighteen-hole golf course opened in 1970. It is a semiprivate club, meaning that it is open to the public, but memberships are available to those who golf enough to need to utilize the fee break membership brings. The course, in combination with the Sports Haven in Novelty, provides the opportunity for classes. In 1989, the officers for the club are Jack Wahl, president, John Wahl, vice president and treasurer, and Al Landi, vice president and secretary.

The Chagrin Valley Athletic Club is located in Bainbridge Township south of State Route 422 on Snyder Road. The original building is a Century Home built in 1852. Don Lybarger bought the house and the land in 1967, and the first part opened in May of that year, with four outdoor tennis courts and outdoor swimming pool. Since then, much has been added including the Cape Cod Dining Room (1969), four more outdoor tennis courts (1970 and 1972), eight indoor tennis courts (1971), the Wimbledon Ballroom (1972), two platform tennis courts and connecting snack bar (1973), indoor pool (1973), a Nautilus area (1980) and a growing Fitness Center. The club suffered a major fire in 1985, but reconstruction has provided one of the finest clubs in northeast Ohio.

These young men from Burton take advantage of a nice spring day and the Civil War encampment at the Century Village in 1989 to do their own re-enactment. They are (in front line from left) Todd Hornak, Peter Frank, Larry Pleva, and Ross Hornak, (against the building from left) Jim Durham, John Jackam, Chris Jackam, and Brian Durham.

Don Tincher has worked at Chardon Lakes Golf Course since 1955. He is presently the manager of the course which was built in 1932. In 1964 the course was expanded from a nine-hole course to eighteen holes. New ownership of the Chardon Lakes area, which is attached to the Bass Lake Development on the outskirts of Chardon, built the new clubhouse behind Don in 1988. The course is open to the public, but there are also memberships available. Early in the history of the course the annual membership fee was $25 per year. 1989 finds membership dues at $660 for an individual for the year.

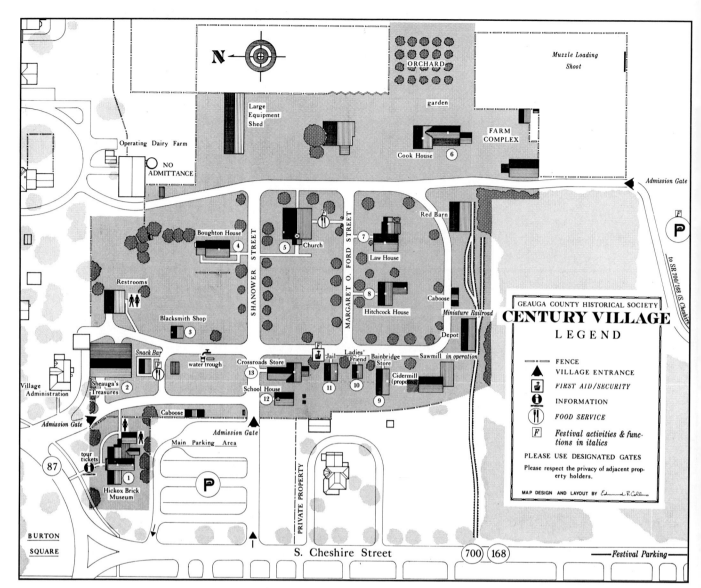

The Century Village is a living outgrowth of the Geauga County Historical Society's interest in preserving the early history of the Western Reserve and a memorial to scores of people who had foresight to lay the groundwork many years ago. Since this map was made there has been one major change to the layout. The blacksmith shop has been moved next to the Red Barn in the depot area to make room for the Munson Town Hall, which was then moved from Fowler's Mills to the Century Village. It now occupies the area across from the water trough, and will serve as the library to house the historical manuscripts and documents which are currently stored in the Hickox Brick Museum. The Historical Society was able to purchase the land including the Hickox Brick thanks to the generous donation of fifteen thousand dollars from the Honorable Frances P. Bolton, congresswoman from Ohio's Twenty-second District. The gift allowed for the purchase of six and one-half acres from Mrs. William Holbury and paid for repairs on the house.
Courtesy of the Geauga County Historical Society

The Crossroads Country Store is a combination of two century-old buildings moved to the Century Village grounds in 1959. The store contains an old-time post office as well as the familiar pot-bellied stove and many household antique items. The store sells the unique products of Geauga County and the Century Village. A fire in 1987 gutted most of the rear of the building, but through the efforts of the Historical Society and generous donations the store was restored.

This railway station and caboose can be found on the Century Village grounds in Burton. The B&O (Baltimore & Ohio) Railroad Station was formerly the Aultman, Ohio, station. It was dismantled and moved from Canton, Ohio, in November 1967. The building was originally built circa 1878. The B&O Caboose is of the series C-I-C399, class CI, initial GCZ and No. 316. It was one of 109 cabooses built in this series between 1913 and 1918 by the B&O Railroad. It is a twenty-ton vehicle which was purchased at Chillicothe, Ohio, moved by rail to Middlefield and was transported to its present location on two flatbed trailer trucks on August 29, 1971.

These triplet kids, owned by Jeff Myers of Montville Township, are taking a break from their tether ball game.
Photograph by Deborah Neiman, Courtesy of the Geauga Times Leader

161

"... OF THE PEOPLE, BY THE PEOPLE, FOR THE PEOPLE.

CHAPTER 10

This aerial photograph shows the Geauga Community Hospital in the early 1960s. At that time the facility had fifty-six beds. The wing to the right was added a few years after the 1959 opening of the hospital.
Photograph by Gene Gehri, courtesy of the Geauga Times Leader

This chapter title "... of the people, by the people, for the people" takes in a scope far broader than government as Mr. Lincoln indicated. The phrase says even more about community. It encompasses government, law enforcement agencies, fire departments, social organizations, libraries, health care professionals (both physical and mental), human service agencies, and anybody who has given his/her time to be with or assist another. Each could have his own chapter, and some their own book, but we can only provide an overview and leave the details for a future project.

GOVERNMENT

In 1989 Geauga County is represented in the U.S. Congress by the two Ohio senators, John Glenn and Howard Metzenbaum, and, as part of the Eleventh U.S. Congressional District by Dennis E. Eckart.

The delegates to the state of Ohio legislature are Robert W. Clark for the Seventy-fourth House District and Charles E. Henry for the Thirty-second Senate District.

The judges serving in Geauga County in 1989 are H. F. Inderlied and Hans Veit in the Court of Common Pleas, Frank G. Lavrich for Probate and Juvenile Court, and Craig S. Albert in Chardon Municipal Court. The jurisdiction for the Municipal Court is all of Geauga County for minor cases, and it holds preliminary hearings for felony cases, then dismisses the alleged criminal or binds them to the County Grand Jury.

County services are supervised by the Board of County Commissioners. The three serving in 1989 are Tony Gall, Edna Davis, and James Mueller.

Other elected county officials and a list of 1989 township and village officials will be included later on in this book.

Each of Geauga County's sixteen townships are served by a board of three trustees and a clerk. The villages of Aquilla, Burton, Chardon, Middlefield, and South Russell each have a village council, mayor, and clerk. Burton also has a Board of Public Affairs, and South Russell additionally has a treasurer.

ORGANIZATIONS

Fraternal orders which have been active at one time or another in the history of Geauga County are: Masonic and Eastern Star Lodges, Knights of Pythias, Knights of Columbus, Maccabees, I.O.O.F. (International Order of Odd Fellows) and Rebekah Lodges, Eagles, D.A.R. (Daughters of the American Revolution), Sons of Temperance, Granges, American Legion, and V.F.W. (Veterans of Foreign Wars).

Social service clubs have included Rotary International, Kiwanis, and Ruritan. Additionally there have been civic associations, cemetery associations, dramatic clubs, mothers clubs, garden clubs, parent-teacher organizations, music clubs, riding clubs, 4-H Clubs, Boy Scouts, Girl Scouts, boys and girls clubs, etc.

These organizations have built buildings, raised funds for worthy projects, marched in parades, and donated time and materials for other projects. But, probably most important of all, they have had fellowship, supported each other during hard times, and had some of the greatest times together known to mankind. They are what community is all about, and they have made Geauga County a much better place to live.

HUMAN SERVICE AGENCIES

Many people might think that law enforcement should be included in the government section, but it truly is a human service agency. Law enforcement in the county is coordinated by the County Sheriff, who, in 1989, is James C. Todd, Ph.D. Although the villages and townships have police departments of their own where possible, the County Sheriff backs up and cooperates with those agencies to promote the best possible service. The Sheriff's Department has also strived to work with the other human services agencies in the county.

Info-Line/Volunteer Bureau was established in the late 1970s with the purpose of providing an information and referral telephone service. In other words, people who called could find out what services to call to solve whatever problems they might have. This service includes crisis intervention, and is linked with Womensafe, (a women's shelter), law enforcement agencies when appropriate, mental health services, and many others. In 1986, Info-Line joined with Geauga County Public Library in a project, funded partially by the State Library of Ohio, to provide access to their files by means of personal computers which were placed in the libraries and other places where people in need could find help sources in a more private way. The Volunteer Bureau half of the agency has served as a facilitator for matching volunteers with public and private agencies. The annual Volunteer Recognition Dinner draws almost two hundred people every year, and they are just the tip of the iceberg of numbers of volunteers that this agency has promoted since its inception.

Mental health services in the county are overseen by the Geauga Community Mental Health Board. Public agencies providing mental health services include Ravenwood Mental Health Center, Catholic Services Bureau, Geauga Family Services (a division of Center for Human Services in Cuyahoga County), New Beginnings, and the Lake-Geauga Center for Alcoholism. In 1987, the Geauga County Mental Health Association was formed through a grant from the Cleveland Foundation and administered by the Community Mental Health Board. The purpose of the association is to provide an independent mental health advocacy group in Geauga County.

Early in 1947 the Geauga Unit of the American Cancer Society drew its first breath at a meeting held in Dr. Alton Behm's office in Chardon. At that meeting were two Field Staff people of the Ohio Division of ACS and Mrs. Loretta (Hausmann) Holmes, president of the Business and Professional Women's Club. As a result, plans were made to launch the first Cancer Fund Drive in Geauga County. Led by Mrs. Holmes, three thousand dollars plus were raised and the Geauga Unit was born and chartered on June 19, 1947. In 1950 the Unit established its first permanent home, an office on South and Water streets in Chardon. Until a secretary, Mary Grieg, was hired in 1956, the entire staff had been volunteers. After several moves called for by expansion, the Geauga Unit is now located on Cherry Street in Chardon. This organization has had some of the most creative fundraising campaigns in the county and state, where it has been recognized as one of the most effective and efficient units. Julie (Sheptak) Armstrong was hired as the first Executive Director in 1963, an office she held for five years.

In 1808, before there was any organization of Chardon Township, Samuel W. Phelps of Painesville was appointed by the Common Pleas Court of Geauga County (the present Lake and Geauga counties comprised Geauga County until 1840) as director to purchase and lay out a town plat for a permanent seat of justice. In that year a one-room log building was constructed to serve as a temporary courthouse. A rude fireplace furnished heat and a split stick and mortar chimney completed this early seat of justice. The builder was Abraham Skinner. The building also served as the jail. (from Pioneer and General History of Geauga County, 1953, page 4) The log cabin pictured was a reconstruction for the 1905 County Centennial Celebration in Chardon.

The Geauga County Court House on Main Street in Chardon preceded the present day courthouse. It was destroyed in the fire on July 25, 1868, which consumed Main Street. The following description is from the Pioneer and General History of Geauga County, 1953. "The Court House had two entrances from Main street, the south entrance being considered the main one. At the left of the south entrance was the Clerk's office, then the Treasurer's office; across the hall were the Auditor's office and the Probate Court. Inside the north entrance at the left was the Recorder's office connected by a door to the Auditor's office. Between the Clerk's and Treasurer's offices were stairs leading to the Court room on the second floor. The jail occupied the north end, the cell room being on the first floor, the next room being known as the debtor's cell. The cellar contained a narrow, dark dungeon. Living quarters for the Sheriff were on the second floor of the jail ... Finishing touches were made to the Court House in 1845 by the enlarging of the cupola and hanging a bell therein."
Courtesy of Kim Glenn

Jim and Sandy Burzanko are standing in front of the Geauga County Pleasant Hill Home where they are the caretakers and every bit care givers as well. In 1839, the county commissioners bought the farm from Nathaniel Stone for twenty-four hundred dollars to be used for a county home. Suitable buildings were then built, and through the years the home has continued to provide a comfortable dwelling for elderly county residents. The home is located in Claridon Township on Aquilla Road between State Route 322 and Butternut Road.

The director in 1989 is Mrs. Donna Lang. Through all this time Mrs. Loretta Mae Holmes has remained a driving force in Geauga County leading hundreds of volunteers in the quest, not only to find a cancer cure, but to provide comfort and support for those afflicted by the disease.

Under the leadership of Info-Line/Volunteer Bureau, the Human Services Forum was established in the early 1980s. This group meets once a month, and is open to all people in the human services agencies in the county from the churches to the police departments. There are relevant presentations at each meeting, but the primary purpose for the group is to keep in touch with each other in order to know about the ongoing and new services provided by the agencies present.

FIRE DEPARTMENTS

Uncontrolled, purposeful and accidental fires have plagued mankind since fire was discovered. Geauga County has had its share of devastating fires including Chardon's Main Street on July 25, 1868, Burton's business district on December 5, 1871, and Parkman's downtown on May 6, 1899. Despite all attempts to make fire-proof facilities and drill fire prevention into people from school-age on, fires continue to disrupt and destroy.

Fire Departments have been established in Bainbridge, Burton, Chardon, Chester, Hambden, Montville, Munson, Newbury, Parkman, Russell, South Russell Village, Thompson, and Troy. Claridon Township does not have a fire department of its own, but contracts with Chardon for protection north of Mayfield Road and Burton for south of Mayfield Road. Huntsburg Township contracts with the Middlefield Fire Department. Combined training sessions among fire departments help to keep costs down and promote consistent action when more than one township are brought together. The Geauga County Firemen's Association was formed in 1944. There is also a chief's association.

Burton Volunteer Fire Department was organized in January 1926. It was incorporated as a nonprofit organization in June 1937.

Chardon organized their Volunteer Fire Department in April 1875. A new organization was established in 1927 to update the equipment and operation.

Fire protection in Chester Township began in 1923 with telephone operator Mrs. Zula Sherman calling businessmen for assistance when a call came. Equipment was purchased in 1925. In October 1943 the Chester Township Fire Department was organized as a nonprofit corporation.

The Munson Fire Department was organized as a nonprofit corporation in March of 1953.

It would be impossible to log the number of

selfless, dangerous, caring, volunteer hours put in by the fire departments and rescue squads in Geauga County. It would also be impossible to thank them adequately.

MEDICINE

The Geauga County Medical Association was organized in 1866. It provided for a consistent scale of fees throughout the county, and it also afforded a close fellowship among the doctors in the county. They shared their discoveries and disappointments. The association met regularly until 1891. It is surmised that increased patient loads and the long horse and buggy rides to Chardon or Burton made the trips hard to justify. The society was reorganized in October of 1905, as the impact of the automobile quickly came to the aid of the doctors. The automobile not only allowed for the resumption of the Medical Association, but it more importantly allowed quicker response to crisis situations, and many more lives were saved.

On February 14, 1921, a banquet was given at the Highland Hotel in Chardon for Dr. Frank S. Pomeroy, who with Dr. Warner of Chesterland was credited with perpetuating the Medical Association. At that banquet, Dr. Pomeroy said, "Forty-two years ago today, a boy of twenty-two years old, who had a raw-boned horse and a buggy, a frayed suit of clothes, $6.25 in money, with ambition and a great deal of conceit, with a buckeye in his pocket, located in Montville to practice medicine. The doctor of today does not occupy the same position that he used to. In the old days, he was advisor in all lines of life, a true friend and counselor. No other position in life affords so complete happiness. There has been a change . . . It is now a financial business."

The statement is probably truer today than in 1921, but Geauga County has had many heroes through the years, from the times of settlement to the present. Many of them have been doctors. The authors encourage the readers to look at the chapter in the 1953 edition of *Pioneer and General History of Geauga County* entitled "Medical." Geauga County has much to be proud of in its medical heritage.

MORE THOUGHTS

The accounts in this chapter don't come close to mentioning all the government officials, organizations, and other public bodies that make Geauga County the community that it is. Our apologies to those we missed in this chapter, especially, for they are every bit as important as the ones we pictured and mentioned.

For county officials not mentioned here, please see the appendix.

Chesterland Brownie Troop 1827 collected dog and cat food for the Geauga County Humane Society. The girls helping to pack are (from the left): Pam Mormino, Jill Zavodny, Deena Laro, and Chris Miscko.

Because of the popularity of 4-H Clubs in Geauga County, Girl Scouting in the county had a slower start than some other areas and began in the late 1930s with lone Troops. From those humble beginnings, Girl Scouting grew rapidly in the decades between 1940 and 1960. The Business and Professional Women's Club invited trainers from the Cleveland Council to come to Geauga to train leaders. In the 1960s the Geauga County Girl Scouts became part of the Cleveland Council. Throughout the years the girls and their leaders have done many community service activities in addition to their camping and other activities.
Photograph by Deborah Naiman, courtesy of the Geauga Times Leader

On Monday, August 20, 1979, Lee Horton (left) and Charles E. McKinney, Jr. (middle) were sworn in as members of the Chardon Police Department. Swearing them in was Mayor and Council President Robert F. Weber. Both officers graduated from the Ohio Peace Officers Training Academy at Lakeland Community College.
Photograph by Marilyn Whipkey, courtesy of the Geauga Times Leader

In 1979 Geauga County received a $287,000 federal grant in the Small Cities Program. Signing the document for the county were (seated from left) Commissioners James Mueller and Richard Ford. Witnessing the signing was Candy Fischer, Community Development Department administrative assistant. The funds were used for emergency repairs and winterizing of homes of the elderly and low income families, sewer projects in Aquilla Village, and home rehabilitation in the Aquilla Village, Kiwanis Lake, Burton Lakes, and Chagrin Falls Park communities.
Courtesy of the Geauga Times Leader

*In October 1979 Munson Township dedicated its new fire station. George Zakany (left), general contractor, stands by as Fire Chief Charles Poutasse takes aim for the ceremonial hose cutting to open the station. Both Mr. Zakany, who died in 1988, and Mr. Poutasse have been very active in the Geauga County community.
Photograph by Marilyn Whipkey, courtesy of the* Geauga Times Leader

*Middlefield Fire Chief Earl Warne (left) looks at a plaque from the Middlefield Chamber of Commerce presented to him in 1979 for fifty years of "Extinguishing" service to the community. Next to Chief Warne is Myron Gibbs and C. J. Ohl is to the right.
Photograph by Doris Cook, courtesy of the* Geauga Times Leader

*Public health Nurse Kay Reckart took the blood pressure reading of Sajar Plastics employee Don Shipman during National High Blood Pressure Month, which was May in 1980. The health department nurses conducted hypertension screenings at various county industries in support of the national event.
Photograph by Bari Stith, courtesy of the* Geauga Times Leader

Art Temple (left), on behalf of Russell Haueter Excavating of Chardon, hands Jim Alvord, treasurer of the Chardon Square Association, a four thousand dollar check to aid in the building costs of the restoration of the bandstand in the Chardon Square. The work was completed soon after this exchange in the fall of 1981. The Chardon Square Association was formed to promote the square and the businesses in the square vicinity. Their decorating of Chardon Square at Christmas with the lighting ceremony and "Days of Christmas Past" celebration, and the Fine Arts Show on the first Sunday in August have become popular annual events drawing people from all over northeastern Ohio.
Photograph by Joseph Koziol, courtesy of the Geauga Times Leader

Mrs. Jesse Hagens of Middlefield and William Luckay of Chardon are all dressed up in Gay Nineties attire for the senior citizens' style show in May of 1980. The show was entitled "Street Walking Through the Decades" and was part of the All-Geauga Senior Citizens Day held at the County Fairgrounds in Burton.

The Geauga County Department on Aging has done an outstanding job of supporting the senior citizens of Geauga County. The offices are located on the lower level of the building which also houses Ravenwood Center on Ravenwood Drive behind the Department of Human Services. The department, under the direction of Mrs. Beebe Eckles until she retired in 1989, provides in-home services, legal assistance, senior day care, and many other activities. The department through its Senior Newsletter, published monthly, identifies programs and activities available to Geauga seniors, as there are several senior clubs throughout the county providing a wide variety of things to do.
Photograph by Sharon Haynes, courtesy of the Geauga Times Leader

Geauga Lyric Theater Guild presented Carousel at the Newbury School Auditorium on Auburn Road on June 20, 21, 27, and 28, 1980. Peter Petersen played Billy Bigelow, and Debbie Plavcan portrayed Julie Jordon.

The Guild had its beginnings at the First Congregational Church of Claridon when members of the choir, assisted by other Geauga County voices, produced the Mikado in September 1954 for a fundraiser. The musical was directed by Robert Dell of Cleveland; the accompanists were Elsie Spurlock (Mrs. Mark) and Ethel Dimmick (Mrs. Alger).
Courtesy of the Geauga Times Leader

On 31 December 1981, Ohio 11th District Court Judge Edwin Hofstetter swore in attorney Fred Green as a new Thompson Township Trustee. This took place in the Chardon Municipal Court. Judge Hofstetter began his law practice in 1959, was elected to the 11th District Court in 1969 and held that post until 1983. In 1989 he is still assigned to the Court of Appeals.
Photograph by Neil Korey, courtesy of the Geauga Times Leader

Two people who have faithfully served Geauga County are Sara Bundus (left) and Judge Robert B. Ford. This photograph was taken on the occasion of their retirement from public office in 1981. Mrs. Bundus had served as Common Pleas Court Bailiff for twenty-one years, and Judge Ford had served as Common Pleas Judge for twenty-eight years. Judge Ford was succeeded by Judge H. F. Inderlied, and Mrs. Bundus was succeeded by Ms. Johanna Diedrich, both of whom continue in their service in 1989.
Photograph by Doris Cook, courtesy of the Geauga Times Leader

Mennonite women from the Middlefield-Mesopotamia area volunteered their time in January 1982 for the Geauga chapter of the American Red Cross bloodmobile stop at the Middlefield First United Methodist Church. Putting together donor blood packets are Priscilla Miller, Susan Byler, JoAnn Kauffman, and Loma Kauffman. There were forty-five volunteers, and 350 pints were collected. The Red Cross chapter not only serves in this way, but also provides training and classes throughout the county for babysitting, CPR (cardio-pulmonary resuscitation), first aid, and similar activities. As always, the American Red Cross is always there where needed for disaster relief.
Photograph by Doris Cook, courtesy of the Geauga Times Leader

Heather Hill Nursing Home resident Ann Ervin (left) shares a letter with volunteer Mildred Collura of Russell. Mrs. Collura serves as a "Friendly Visitor" at the Chardon facility in this 1982 photograph. Geauga County is blessed with six fine and caring nursing homes including the Pleasant Hill Home in Claridon, Briar Hill in Middlefield, Holly Hill and Maple Nursing Homes in Newbury Township, Blossom Hill in Huntsburg, Heather Hill in Munson Township, and Quality Care in Chardon. The county is also fortunate to have an assisted living center for senior citizens in Montville. This center called Geauga Assisted Living provides a place for senior citizens who still want to do for themselves but need some assistance in doing so.
Courtesy of the Geauga Times Leader

This building was the new Post Office in Chardon when it opened April 1, 1940. It functioned as such until 1986 when it was purchased by the Board of Trustees of the Geauga County Public Library to serve as the Administrative Center for the library system. It now houses the audio-visual, technical services, special county-wide services including the bookmobile, as well as the administrative staff for the four community libraries and the Thompson Library Station located in Ledgemont High School. Ms. Nancy Marietta has been the librarian at Thompson since the library station began in 1979. The community libraries are in Chardon, Bainbridge, Chesterland, and Middlefield. Directors for the Geauga County Public Library since it was designated a district County Library have been Harriet Johnson, Marjorie Ramisch, G. W. Stanbery, Terry McLaughlin, Sieglinde Williams, Stephen Kershner, and Lawrence J. Corbus. In 1989, the Board of Trustees for Geauga County Public Library are Betty Chorman, Sandra Werft, Sister Mary Aimee, Mona Trybus, Donald Cornish, Anderson Allyn, Sr., and Paul Newman. Helen Wilson of Chardon has been Clerk-Treasurer since January 1970.

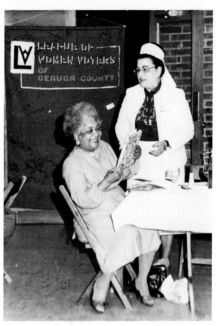

Geauga Community Hospital President Paul C. Jacobs (center), Pediatrics Head Nurse Anna Jane Hult (right) and child-life worker Marilyn Fox look over the three winning entries in the hospital's Children and Hospital's Week poster contest held in April 1982. The winners were Karen Elliot of Burton (three to five year-olds), Betsy Corrigan (six to nine year-olds) and Maria Toogood (ten to twelve year-olds). Mr. Jacobs through his years of outstanding service to the community has been the primary leader in the tremendous development and growth of the Geauga Hospital.
Courtesy of the Geauga Times Leader

In 1982, Geneva Maiden (seated) was presented a gift of appreciation by Helen Jesse, president of the League of Women Voters of Geauga County. Maiden was recognized for her service as president and treasurer of the local chapter, secretary of the board, nominating committee of the national board, and chairwoman of the national committee to increase minority outreach. Appropriately this dinner was held in Chesterland, where the Geauga County League of Women Voters got its start on May 17, 1947.
Courtesy of the Geauga Times Leader

Terry Harrington, B. J. Shanower, Helen Burns, and Alice Ferris admire the Bicentennial quilt designed by the late Gertrude Thayer for the Geauga County Historical Society.

The ladies belong to the Sheauga Quilters Guild. In 1983, the guild started a maintenance fund for the Burton Museum's quilt collection. During the summer of 1987, the Progress-Research quilt (pictured on the dust jacket) was placed under the care of the guild.

Every Tuesday is quilting day at the historical society. The quilt that is made is raffled off at the annual quilt show which is held in May.
Photograph by Doris Cook, courtesy of the Geauga Times Leader

The Burton Public Library was established by the Civic Improvement Society in 1910. From its first home above Crittenden Drug Store on Main Street it moved in 1912 to the Johnson Store building. It moved to its present location, the second high school, in 1937. The original building was built in 1884, and a major renovation and addition were completed in 1983. When the Geauga County Public Library was formed in 1963, the Burton Public Library Board of Trustees chose not to join and kept the library as an independent school district library. Community librarians have been Miss Mary Andrews, Miss Abbey Tolles, Mrs. Charles Dow, Mrs. Josie Street, Mrs. Caroline E. Boak (first trained librarian), Mrs. Helen Merritt, and Mrs. Carol Varga. In 1989 the Board of Trustees of the Burton Library is comprised of Mrs. Pat Braunlich, Mrs. Jean Dively, Mrs. Kathy Johnson, Charles Head, Vince Kelleher, Tim Matlock and Paul Miller. The clerk-treasurer in 1989 is Ms. Marilyn Pickett. The library shares the building with Burton Village which maintains its office on the second floor, and the Burton Police Department is located in the basement.
Photograph by David Holzheimer, courtesy of the Burton Public Library.

Friends of the Bainbridge Library and trustees of the Geauga County Public Library met October 3, 1981, to unveil a sign designating the location of the new Bainbridge Library, which was to be moved from a storefront on Washington Street. The site at the northwest corner of the intersection of State Route 422 and Snyder Road is centrally located to serve the communities of Auburn, Bainbridge, and South Russell. Assembled are (left to right): Auburn Township Trustee Elmer Cross, community Librarian Tim Kassinger, library Trustees Carol Miller and Sister Mary Aimee of Notre Dame Academy, Friends' President Barbara Miner, and library Trustees Don Cornish, Betty Chorman, Mona Trybus, and Evelyn Williams.
Photograph by Deborah Sekerak, courtesy of the Geauga Times Leader

The Middlefield Library was established in 1942. In the 1960s, it was located in limited space in a house and storefront on High Street just west of Middlefield Junior High School. In 1973 the existing buildings were razed, and a new library was built on the same site. The books were housed in the Village Hall across the street while the new facility was being built. The community librarians since the 1960s have been Mary Crowe, Anne Maroush, Mary Cleland, and Mary Fran Gumpper. The library is part of the Geauga County Public Library.

The Bainbridge Branch Library was established in 1965 and housed in a storefront on Washington Street in Bainbridge west of State Route 306. The new Bainbridge Library opened in August of 1985 approximately two miles east to the northwest corner of Snyder Road and Washington Street (State Route 422). Community librarians have been Mrs. Bobbie Mosenthal, Mrs. Dorothy Stinson, Mr. Tim Kassinger, and Mrs. Holly Carroll. The library is part of the Geauga County Public Library.

The Chardon Public Library was organized on August 26, 1848, with John French, County Recorder, being chosen librarian. It was housed in the recorder's office and administered as an association library with a membership fee of one dollar per year. In 1882, the library was moved to a building on the village square. The library history for the 1890s is missing, but in 1898 a small reading group, which became the Progress Literary Club the next year, was formed. This organization became the parent of the local library. At this time the collection was housed and loaned from private homes, but increased demand for adequate housing effected the move to the county courthouse. In 1910 the Progress Club turned over the use and management of the book collection to the village government but retained ownership, and the books were moved to the village hall. The first library board was appointed in 1913, and Mrs. Mary Radcliffe served as a board member, attendant and assistant until her retirement in 1947. In 1915 a lot was purchased to accommodate a Carnegie Library, but World War I and increased costs prevented the utilization of the Carnegie grant, and the lot was sold in 1921. The library became a district County Library on July 9, 1963, and the main library of Geauga County Public Library. In 1970 the library was moved to its present location at 110 East Park Street. Community librarians have been Mrs. Ruth Daniels, Miss Harriet Ely Johnson, Miss Marjorie Ramisch, Mrs. Sieglinde Williams, Mr. Lawrence J. Corbus, and Mr. James J. Anderson. In 1987 the administration of the Geauga County Public Library was moved to 121 South Street allowing the sixteen thousand square foot building to be renovated in 1987-1988 and utilized entirely for library public service area.

Workmen are putting the finishing touches on the Geauga West Library in Chesterland which opened the end of May 1989. Its predecessor, the Chester Branch Library, was established in 1957, and, as a part of Geauga County Public Library, grew under the leadership of community Librarians Mary Eykyn, Marjorie Ramisch, Esther Saunders, Holly Carroll, and Cynthia Orr. The library began on Mayfield Road, moved to a site on the corner of Chillicothe and Mayfield roads (State Routes 306 and 322), then to Herrick Drive where it stayed from 1970 until 1989. Through the help of the West Geauga Board of Education, which donated the land, and the passing of a bond levy by the community in 1986, the administration and the Board of Trustees of Geauga County Public Library were able to carry out the construction of this building. The architect was David Holzheimer and Associates of Geauga County.

The changes in just thirty years to the Geauga Hospital have been astounding. The hospital now contains approximately 170 beds. Although it is considered a primary care facility, there are many services. They include many wellness programs as well as the traditional hospital services. Several examples of those programs are: Nutricise (led by the dietitian and physical therapists); Smoke Stoppers; Cardiac Club (education and support); I Can Cope (living with cancer); Lamaze/Pre-Natal Classes; Chemical Dependency Unit and many others. The most impressive part of the hospital is the caring staff and volunteers who make difficult situations quite a lot better. In 1989 the President and Chief Executive Officer for the Geauga Hospital is Richard J. Frenchie. Courtesy of Geauga Hospital

This modern Post Office for Chardon was completed in 1986. The Post Office at Chardon was established December 5, 1814, with Edward Paine, Jr., as the first postmaster. In 1880 the Post Office was moved to No. 10 Union Block and located in the rear of A.D. Hovey's Drug Store. The first postmaster after the office became authorized by presidential appointment in 1882 was W. C. Parsons. In 1886 the Post Office was moved to No. 2 Randall Block. When Henry Bickle added another store building to his property in the north section of the business block, the Post Office was moved to that location in 1903. On April 1, 1940, a new Post Office building was opened at the corner of South Street and Randall Court. The postal service remained there until 1986, and that building now houses the administrative offices of the Geauga County Public Library. (Pre-1950 information is excerpted from Pioneer and General History of Geauga County, 1953, pages 309 and 310)

This new county youth home on Aquilla Road in Claridon Township, across from the Geauga County Home for the aged was completed in 1989 to replace the Pope Home, in Troy Township, which was rendered unusable by vandalism and fire. Lewis L. Pope had presented his large brick mansion and 120-acre estate to the people of the county in October 1933. It had been the Pope family homestead since 1818.

175

LOOSE ENDS

This fine pair of mules stands ready for work in the early part of the century. If size of ears are any indication of strength, these were two strong mules.
Courtesy of Shetler Printing/Roose Drug

CHAPTER 11

As the reader can probably guess from the chapter title, the authors needed to tie up some loose ends. As information was garnered for this tome, we found some topics that we thought were special, or interesting, or didn't really fit in other areas. Even with these items, there will always be more to share about Geauga County.

The village fires that affected the county, although devastating and tragic at the time, brought some healthy changes to the communities. Hence, some additional street scenes are included.

TELEPHONE COMPANIES

The first telephone lines in Ohio were erected in Burton in 1877. Over the years each community developed its own telephone system and, hence, small independent companies. The Burton Telephone Company was purchased by Ohio Bell Telephone Company in May 1927. The Chardon Telephone Company, organized in 1895, later became the Western Reserve Telephone Company, and still later Alltel. By the 1980s, the county telephone lines had become divided into either Alltel or Ohio Bell. One of the problems that exists in the county is that long distance telephone calls aren't all that long in distance because of two service companies. It is possible in the county to have, for example, a Burton telephone number and a Chardon mailing address.

POLITICS

If there ever was a county where being a Republican was hereditary, it was probably Geauga County. Although the difference is not as great now, the Republican heritage in the county runs deep and long. Before the Republican party as it stands came about, there were the Free Soil Party and the Whigs. Very much the Abolitionists, there was never any doubt on which side of the Civil War Geauga Countians stood.

National political rivalries have not been the only political rivalries that have occurred in the county. Early in the development of the county government, a push came from Burton to have the county seat there because of its central location. The negative feelings that developed between the two villages at that time ran so deep, that they are still evident in 1989, over 150 years later. East Claridon and Claridon Center drew their lines along religious boundaries, Methodist and Congregationalist. Auburn Center and Auburn Corners feuded for where their town hall should be located.

Fortunately, most of the bitter feelings have passed, and the occasions for working together for the common good have far exceeded the times of rifts.

MEDIA

The newspaper business in Geauga County has not been an easy business. In the early years neighborhood news dominated. It was important to know who was sick, who died, who was away on vacation, and who was visiting from out of town. The first newspaper in the county was the *Chardon Spectator and Geauga Gazette* in the 1830s. It lasted only a few years. The *Geauga Freeman* appeared in Chardon in 1840, and, before its move to Cleveland in 1854, had a name change to *Geauga Republican and Whig*. The *Free Democrat*, which was the forerunner of the *Geauga Republican* began in December 1849. In 1854, the *Free Democrat* became the *Jeffersonian Democrat*, then, the *Geauga Democrat* (1866), and finally, the *Geauga Republican* (1872). Hard times compelled mergers resulting in the *Geauga Republican-Record*. The *Geauga Record* had been printed in Burton.

The 1890s had seen the *Middlefield Messenger* arrive. In 1903 it became the *Middlefield Times*. The Burton *Geauga Leader* had taken over the printing of the *Middlefield Times,* and, in 1942, they formed the *Geauga Times Leader*. The *Geauga News* which lasted from 1922 to 1944 in Chardon joined with the *Republican-Record*. 1949 saw the end of the *Republican-Record.*

After all of this confusion, we find in 1989 the *Geauga Times Leader* published in Chardon. The *Good News,* published by Shetler Printing in Middlefield, contains personal messages and classified advertisements, and serves the southeastern quadrant of the county. The *Weekly Mail* is published in Chardon, contains strictly local news and classified, and has a *Messenger* edition which reaches to other parts of Geauga County. The *Chagrin Valley Times* serves mostly the Bainbridge area. For many years the *Chesterland News* served that area, but unfortunately ceased publication in the mid-1980s.

Radio and television service to Geauga County has mostly come from Cleveland stations. The exception to this has been the locally owned WBKC AM radio station established in Chardon. It moved to Painesville, but the station facility was taken over by WCDN AM. That station still operates in 1989 from Chardon. FM radio station WPHR 108 began in Newbury in the early 1980s, but it moved to Cleveland in 1988. Geauga County hills have often posed reception problems in receiving Cleveland radio and television stations, but, depending on which side of a hill you live, Pittsburgh, Wheeling, Erie, and Canadian stations could come in very well. In the middle of the 1980s Cablevision of Geauga County brought cable television, which, in 1989, serves Chardon, Burton, and Middlefield. The western portion of the county is served by cable television from Cuyahoga County.

LITERATURE

The most prolific and widely known author to come from Geauga County was Albert Gallatin Riddle. He was approximately one year old when he came with his family from Massachusetts to Newbury in 1817. His father died in 1823, leaving his mother and other relatives to help in the raising of eight boys and one girl. Eventually he became a lawyer after years of study in the law office of Seabury Ford. He was active in the Whig party, but even a stronger supporter of rights for Negroes. He gained national prominence and supported President Lincoln. He maintained a law office in Washington, D.C., known for his support of Negro rights. His works of fiction and history drew from his Geauga County upbringing, as he used local settings for his novels. Ansel's cave, on the property of American Society for Metals, served that purpose in his book, *Ansel's Cave*. Mr. Riddle died in 1902.

Geauga County is fortunate in 1989 to have two outstanding poets residing in the county. Ms. Grace Butcher, a Claridon resident, has had her work published in many journals throughout her career. In addition, she has produced several books including *Rumors of ecstasy . . . rumors of death,* and *Before I go out on the road.* She is an English professor at the Geauga Campus of Kent State University.

Mr. Hale Chatfield is also well known in poetry circles. As an English professor at Hiram College, the Huntsburg resident is a popular lecturer. His works include "The Young Country" and other poems, and "At Home," plus numerous entries in nationally known poetry journals. He received a National Endowment for the Humanities fellowship in 1975 and an Ohio Arts Council fellowship in 1980.

One of the exciting happenings in Geauga County in the 1980s is the encouragement of youth creative writing as evidenced in the Young Authors programs that take place throughout the county. Authors from all over the country have come to Geauga County to share with and guide the children in their efforts. The Geauga County Board of Education, the school systems, and the public libraries have been instrumental in carrying out this worthy endeavor.

HISTORICAL SOCIETIES

The Geauga County Historical Society has been cited throughout this book for its great contributions to Geauga County life.

Additionally, individual communities have developed their own historical and preservation societies to hold on to the rich heritage that is here.

The Chesterland Historical Society has developed the Chester Historical Park on the corner of Caves and Mayfield roads. The Middlefield Historical Society has restored the Century Inn built by James Thompson in 1818, and it serves the community by collecting, preserving, and disseminating knowledge of the history of Middlefield and the surrounding area. Auburn and Parkman have made similar inroads. The Chardon Preservation Society was formed to try to protect the old high school on the square in Chardon from demolition. Although unsuccessful in that endeavor, they brought the attention of the community to the need for stewardship of its heritage. It continues to collect articles, photographs, and manuscripts reflecting that heritage.

The Geauga County Genealogical Society has developed the reputation for being one of the finest such organizations in the United States. Through thousands of volunteer hours the society has organized, indexed, and preserved Probate records, marriage, birth, death, and cemetery records. The Anderson Allyn Room for Genealogical Research in the Chardon Library provides an excellent place for the research, thanks to the volunteers who are so dedicated to its excellence.

SMITH PHOTOGRAPHS

Some coincidences occurred while the determination that a pictorial history would be a feasible undertaking. On the day that the publisher's representative, Mr. Jim Williams, came to Chardon to meet with Teeter Grosvenor and Jim Anderson, Jim A. returned to the library and received a call from Mrs. Virginia Carlburg in California. She said that she was a retired librarian, whose father had been born and raised in Chardon. Her father, Murray Sterling Smith had been an amateur photographer in his youth, and she thought that it would be appropriate that the glass plate negatives he had left to her should be returned to Geauga County. His father, Stuart Smith had built the house in 1897 which was razed in 1969 to make room for the Geauga County Public Library. Two months later, the contract to write the book was signed, and that afternoon, Mrs. Carlburg called again to say that the plates were on their way. In fairness to a county-wide project, it was felt that only a few of the photos could be included, and they are. The family story that Mrs. Carlburg shared was inspiring, and the gift she gave to the county in the photos will be cherished for years to come. Our heartfelt thanks go to her, and the many other people who have touched Geauga County, cared about Geauga County, and worked to preserve the history and heritage which can provide inspiration and vision for the future.

This is Main Street in Chardon before the fire, which occurred on July 25, 1868, destroying all of the buildings pictured. Courtesy of Kim Glenn

The rebuilding of Chardon was undertaken by contractors, Messrs. Herrick and Simmons of Cleveland, and they began in the fall of 1868. Pictured are the workmen on the Randall Block, which is at the south end of Main Street. The rebuilding of Main Street was completed by midwinter, 1869.
Courtesy of Mrs. Dorothy (Parsons) Knapp

The proprietors in the Opera House Block take advantage of a photographer on Main Street in Chardon circa 1882. From left to right, they are: Dr. Pem Cowles, unknown, Harry Bickle, Steve Griffith (seated), Horace Hammond, and Henry Bickle.
Courtesy of Anderson Allyn

Peter Guren, who is a resident of Huntsburg, is the creator of the syndicated newspaper cartoon character, Shagg. The Ask Shagg comic strip is designed to answer questions about animals that children (of all ages) have. Peter is pictured here with another favorite character, Shamu, the killer whale of Sea World, which is located on Geauga Lake.
Courtesy of United Media

The Exchange Hotel was built in 1843 on the site of the Umberfield Tavern on the corner of West Park and West Center Streets in Burton. It was so named because mail carriers traveling between Painesville and Marietta would exchange their horses there. It became the only four-story building in the county. In the late 1870s, it became the "Temperance Hotel." It later became the Burton Hotel. Still later it became a rooming house. It was condemned and torn down in 1942.
Courtesy of Stanlae Merritt

Burton's Main Street looked like this in 1860. It was destroyed by fire on December 5, 1871. Courtesy of Shetler Printing/ Roose Drug

"Ask Shagg" by Peter Guren of Huntsburg is seen in two hundred newspapers all over the country and enjoyed by kids of all ages.
Reprinted by Permission of United Feature Syndicate, Inc.

This is a view from the park of the east side of Main Street in Burton prior to the paving of the streets and parking.
Courtesy of Shetler Printing/Roose Drug

Nearing completion in the spring of 1989 is the Thompson Ledges Park Museum. This museum is located at the site of the former William Gilbert Hotel on the edge of the park lands. It has been built through the generous donation of Alexander J. Zebehazy of Painesville in honor of his late wife, Margaret McLean Zebehazy. Mrs. Zebehazy's family had settled in Thompson on the land where Ledgemont High School stands.

The end of World War I was certainly reason enough to celebrate in Burton. This happy group gathered in front of Park's Pharmacy which was located on the east side of Main Street at the square.
Courtesy of Carl Mowery

This is Parkman before the fire in 1899.
Courtesy of Shetler Printing/Roose Drug

As was the case with most fires that have occurred in Geauga County, the Parkman fire of 1899 was devastating. Believed to have been started by spontaneous combustion, W.H. Cromwell found the second story of his grocery and drugstore on fire. In addition to Mr. Cromwell's loss were Dave Mace's shoe shop, the Blackmarr office building, the general store and millinery owned by Mr. and Mrs. E. J. Percival, and parts of the stores owned by A. C. Weygant and Charles Bundy. The wooden buildings were replaced with brick soon after the fire.
Courtesy of Shetler Printing/Roose Drug

On July 4, 1932, an elm tree, descended from the tree under which George Washington took command of the Continental Army on July 3, 1775, was planted and dedicated next to the Geauga County Court House in Chardon. The Boy Scouts, Campfire Girls, Childs-Taylor Chapter of the D.A.R. (Daughters of the American Revolution), and prominent citizens took part in that dedication. (Courtesy of the Geauga Times Leader) A plaque commemorating the occasion was embedded in a stone at the base of the tree. (Photograph by Jill Coder-Sestak, courtesy of the Geauga Times Leader) On April 29, 1989, the Bicentennial of the Constitution Committee of Geauga County refurbished the plaque and rededicated the tree, which still thrives despite the periodic tortures of Geauga County weather. This culminated the three years of activities of commemoration by the Committee. In addition, trees representing the townships in Geauga County were planted along the north driveway of the Geauga County Fair Grounds. That dedication also took place on April 29, 1989, and it symbolized the patriotism and stewardship which have characterized the people of Geauga County throughout their history. (Courtesy of Edna Davis)

BIBLIOGRAPHY

Bushman, Jane and Gloria Jean Leagan. *To Munson with Love.* Chardon, Ohio: Bushman and Leagan, 1976.

Warren, Violet and Jeannette Grosvenor. *A Monumental Work; Inscriptions and Interments in Geauga County, Ohio through 1983.* Evansville, Indiana: Whipporwill Publications, 1985.

Howe, Henry. *Historical Collections of Ohio in two volumes.* Cincinnati, Ohio: C. J. Krehbiel & Co., 1888.

Pioneer and General History of Geauga County. Geauga County, Ohio: The Historical Society of Geauga County, 1880.

Pioneer and General History of Geauga County. Evansville, Indiana: The Geauga County Historical and Memorial Society, 1953.

Downes, Randolph C. *History of Lake Shore Ohio.* 3 vols. New York: Lewis Historical Publishing Co., Inc., 1952.

Geauga County Planning Commission. *Industrial Directory of Geauga County, Ohio 1986.* Chardon, Ohio. 1986.

History of Geauga and Lake Counties, Ohio. Philadelphia: Williams Brothers, 1878.

Lake Erie Girl Scout Council the First Seventy-five Years; a Council History, 1912 - 1987. Cleveland, Ohio, 1987.

Wheeler, Robert A. "Land and Community in Rural Nineteenth Century America: Claridon Township, 1810-1870." *Ohio History.* Volume 97/Summer-Autumn 1988. pp.101-121.

Pictured is Public Square and Main Street in Parkman circa 1908.
Courtesy of Shetler Printing/Roose Drug

One of the pleasures in developing this pictorial history was the gift of Mrs. Virginia Carlburg of the glass plate negatives and some original prints taken by her father, Murray S. Smith, when he was a boy growing up in Chardon, Ohio, at the turn of the century. He photographed the world as he saw it. Because of the additional beauty of his handwriting, we want to share a sample of captions.
Courtesy of Mrs. Virginia Carlburg

Appendix 1

Population Statistics

The 1990 Federal Census will soon begin. Unfortunately, it will miss the personal touch of the census taker who went house to house. Most were paid by the number of names entered in the ledger. One unscrupulous enumerator copied names from tombstones (not in Geauga County, however) because the count determined legislative representation. The 1870 Census in Geauga County was considered inaccurate. The residents petitioned the Census Bureau for a recount which was granted. The count was done in 1871 and resulted in over eleven hundred names being added.

The current system is called "Random Sampling." In it a researcher would lose the neighborhood concept and who "the girl next door" is. The following comes from a report available through the Geauga County Public Library system.

TOTALS & MEDIANS

	1980 CENSUS	1988 ESTIMATE	1980-1988	%CHANGE 1993 PROJECTION
Total Population	74,474	75,799	1.8	76,922
Total Households	22,880	24,679	7.9	25,740
Household Population	73,905	75,230	1.8	76,353
Average Household Size	3.2	3.0	-5.6	3.0
Average Household Income	$28,442	$42,612	49.8	$51,920
Median Household Income	$24,384	$35,298	44.8	$43,131

TOTALS IN VARIOUS CATEGORIES IN 1980

	TOTAL	(0-4)	(15)	(65+)	(75+)	(85+)
Female Population	37,410	2,788	9,605	3,207	1,215	349
Male Population	37,064	2,913	10,137	2,375	684	134

POPULATION BY RACE

WHITE	73,133
BLACK	990
HISPANIC	305
OTHER	351

INDUSTRY

Agr/Forest/Fish/Mining	983
Construction	2,527
Manufacturing/Nondurable	3,521
Manufacturing/Durable	7,670
Transportation	855
Communications	704
Wholesale Trade	1,371
Retail Trade	4,922
Finance/Insurance/Real Estate	1,567
Business/Repair Service	1,231
Pesonnel/Entertainment/Records	1,148
Health Service	2,317
Educational Service	2,678
Other Professional Related Ser.	1,310
Public Adminstration	795
Total Employed	33,599

OCCUPATION

Managerial	4,441
Professional	4,407
Technical	944
Admin/Clerical	4,688
Sales	3,463
Household Service	202
Protective Service	393
Other Service	2,737
Farm/Forests/Fish	878
Product/Craft/Repair	5,634
Machine Operators	3,159
Transportation/Moving	1,436
Handlers/Cleaners	1,217
	33,599

MEANS OF TRANSPORTATION TO WORK

Drive/Carpool	30,135
Public Transportation	561
Other	2,043

TRAVEL TIME TO WORK

0 - 14 minutes	8,163
15 - 29 minutes	9,290
30 - 59 minutes	12,443
60 + minutes	1,779

EDUCATION OF ADULTS OVER 25 YEARS OF SCHOOL COMPLETED

0 - 11 years	9,866	23.3%
12 years	16,793	39.7%
13 - 15 years	6,969	16.5%
16 + years	8,696	20.5%
Median Years Completed		12.7

MARITAL STATUS

	Male	%	Female	%
Single	7,148	26.5	5,902	21.2
Married	18,166	67.5	18,166	65.3
Separated	144	0.5	206	0.7
Widowed	496	1.8	2,239	8.1
Divorced	973	3.6	1,292	4.6

POPULATION BY TOWNSHIP AND VILLAGE

The 1980 figures were given by the Geauga County Planning Commission as final counts from the Federal Census Bureau as of 28 Apr 1981.

The Fact Book is published annually by the *Times-Leader* in January or February. The issue of Friday, 27 Jan 1989, has the population (as reported in the most recent census), various officers, meeting dates and times, and phone numbers.

BURTON TOWNSHIP

Population:	Township	Village
1960	1,920	1,085
1970	2,366	1,214
1980	2,779	1,401

MIDDLEFIELD TOWNSHIP

Population:	Township	Village
1960	2,063	1,467
1970	2,738	1,726
1980	3,572	1,997

THOMPSON TOWNSHIP

Population:	Township
1960	1,369
1970	1,834
1980	2,083

CHESTER TOWNSHIP

Population:	Township
1960	6,566
1970	10,388
1980	11,212

HAMBDEN TOWNSHIP

Population:	Township
1960	1,764
1970	2,494
1980	2,934

PARKMAN TOWNSHIP

Population:	Township
1960	1,782
1970	2,054
1980	2,638

HUNTSBURG TOWNSHIP

Population:	Township
1960	1,481
1970	1,792
1980	2,201

NEWBURY TOWNSHIP

Population:	Township
1960	3,719
1970	4,038
1980	5,337

TROY TOWNSHIP

Population:	Township
1960	1,554
1970	1,652
1980	1,735

CLARIDON TOWNSHIP

Population:	Township	Aquilla Village
1960	2,320	
1970	2,124	389
1980	2,457	355

BAINBRIDGE TOWNSHIP

Population:	Township
1960	5,423
1970	7,038
1980	8,207

CHARDON TOWNSHIP

Population:	Township	Village
1960	2,056	3,154
1970	3,180	3,991
1980	3,537	4,370

AUBURN TOWNSHIP

Population:	Township
1960	1,451
1970	1,587
1980	2,351

MONTVILLE TOWNSHIP

Population:	Township
1960	1,216
1970	1,307
1980	1,722

MUNSON TOWNSHIP

Population:	Township	
1960	2,460	
1970	3,569	
1980	5,222	Chardon Village part - 64

RUSSELL TOWNSHIP

Population:	Township	Hunting Valley Village	South Russell Village
1960	4,644		
1970	4,545	124	2,673
1980	5,363	153	2,784

Appendix 2

School Population by District
GEAUGA COUNTY SCHOOLS
Enrollment 15 Oct 1988

	Grades	Students	Total
BERKSHIRE			
High School	7-12	618	
Burton Elementary	K-6	352	
Claridon Elementary	K-6	191	
Troy Elementary	K-6	163	
			1,324
CARDINAL			
High School	9-12	397	
Middle School	7-8	211	
Huntsburg Elementary	K-6	196	
Jordak Elementary	K-6	515	
Parkman Elementary	K-6	231	
			1,550
CHARDON			
High School	9-12	874	
Middle School	6-7-8	594	
Hambden Elementary	K-5	158	
Maple Elementary	K-5	373	
Munson Elementary	K-5	368	
Park Elementary	K-5	309	
			2,676
KENSTON			
High School	9-12	795	
Middle School	6-7-8	514	
Intermediate School	4-5	317	
Auburn Elementary	3	174	
Gardiner Elementary	K-1-2	562	
			2,362
LEDGEMONT			
High School	9-12	225	
Elementary	K-8	533	
			758
NEWBURY			
High School	7-12	401	
Elementary	K-6	505	
			906
WEST GEAUGA			
High School	9-12	907	
Middle School	6-7-8	487	
Lindsey	K-5	479	
Westwood	K-5	414	
			2,287
			11,863

Courtesy of the Geauga County Board of Education

Appendix 3

Geauga County Officials

PROSECUTOR
DAVID P. JOYCE, 16575 Wren Road, Chagrin Falls, OH 44022

COMMISSIONERS
TONY GALL, 16878 Valley Drive, Mantua, OH 44255
JAMES MUELLER, 7939 Kinsman Road, Novelty, OH 44072
EDNA L. DAVIS, 15973 Johnson Street, Middlefield, OH 44062

AUDITOR
RICHARD J. MAKOWSKI, 12811 Aquilla Rd., Chardon OH 44024

TREASURER
JOHN A. CRAVENS, 10690 Wilson Mills Road, Chardon, OH 44024

CLERK OF COURTS
BETTY J. MONTAGUE, 8375 Wilson Mills Road, Chesterland, OH 44026

RECORDER
CATHERINE H. HEIDEN, 12185 Clark Road, Chardon, OH 44024

ENGINEER
R. L. PHILLIPS, 11551 Wilbert Road, Chardon, OH 44024

CORONER
ALBERT EVANS, 14830 Orchard Avenue, Middlefield, OH 44062

SHERIFF
JAMES C. TODD, 13041 Millstone Drive, Chardon, OH 44024

"Mary T. Smith and Etta Sanger in the hiring Room of the old B. B. Woodbury House taken in 1897–1898. Was taken with my second Camera with 2½ x 2½ glass plates. "We lived in the "Woodbury House" for about 3 years before moving into the new House that my Father built in the Park in 1898."—M.S.S.
Courtesy of Mrs. Virginia Carlburg

INDEX

A
Abolitionists 177
abstainers 29
Accessibility 43
accountant 192
Action Photographers 117
Adams, Paul 112
adopting a tree 63
advisor 167
aerial 163
agencies 166
aging 170; Dept. on 170
agricultural property 78
agriculture 29, 75-95, 127, 128
Aikens, Robert 63
Aimee, Sister Mary 172, 173
Air Show 125
aircraft carrier 125
airports 117
Akron (OH) 12, 104, 108; Bureau of Water Supply 15
Akron Watershed 12
Alaska 110
Albert, Craig S. 163
Alcoholism 164
Alderman, Grace Armena 34
Aletheia (Truth) 50
Alexander, Charles 130
Alliance, OH 192
Alltel 177
Allyn, Anderson, Jr. "Spike" 137
Allyn, Anderson, Sr. 7, 64, 108, 137, 142, 179, 180
Alpine Valley 74, 151
aluminum 137; tubing 140
Alvord, Jim 170
American Cancer Society 7, 164
American Legion 164; Hall 71
American Red Cross 171
American Society for Metals 140, 178
Amish 24, 40, 53, 54, 60, 77, 78, 82, 83, 86, 87, 107, 125, 127, 133, 143, 155; Old Order 40, 78
Amish education 59
Amish schools 69
Amish-Dutch 87
Ammonn, Jakob 78
amusement parks 146
Anabaptists 78
Anderson Allyn Room for Genealogical Research 179
Anderson, Adam James 192
Anderson, Christopher John 192
Anderson, Elizabeth (Short) 192
Anderson, James J. "Jim" 137, 152, 174, 179, 192
Anderson, Sarah Elizabeth 192
Andrews, Elosia 31
Andrews, Irma 67
Andrews, Mary 173
animals 11, 19, 85, 180
Anniversary 123
Ansel Road 70
Ansel's Cave 12, 178
Anspach, Bob 125
anthology 63
apertures 32
apothecary 141
apple/s 87; butter 87; cider 127
Apple Butter Festival 22, 87, 89, 145, 155
AppleWorks 30
appliance/s 137; industry 141
Aquila 37
Aquilla 146; Lake 12; Road 30, 150, 165, 175; Village (OH) 37, 163, 184
architect 174
Armstrong, Gloria 61
Armstrong, Julia/Julie (Sheptak) 7, 56, 164
Armstrong, William H., Rev. 41
ARSENIC AND OLD LACE 65
arsonist 80
asbestos 69
ash tree 98
ashes 107
Ashtabula 74, 116; County 20, 27, 28, 35, 74, 138
Ask Shagg 180
Askew, Mildred 50
Aspen Grove Picnic Area 18
Assembly of God 51, 52, 70
assisted living center 171
Aster, Ferdl 151
"At Home" 178
attorney 132, 171
Atwood, Don 63
Auburn (OH) 11, 12, 32, 35, 47, 66, 81, 82, 119, 127, 129, 151, 173, 178, 184
Auburn Alumni Association 66
Auburn Center 35, 116, 177
Auburn Community Church 47
Auburn Corners 35, 116, 177
Auburn Grade School 66
Auburn Hunting Area 146
Auburn Road 36, 116, 124, 141, 146, 179
Auburn Springs Golf Course 146
auction 55
audio-visual services 172
auditor 185
auditor's office 165
augers 98
Aultman (OH) 161
Aurora (OH) 32
Austintown (OH) 32
authors 178
automobile/s 78, 116, 126, 167
automotive 137, 141
autos 108
Avery's Store 136
Avery, B. F., Judge 126
ax/e 99, 115
azaleas 78

B
Babbish, Albert 62
Babbish, Helen 62
babysitting 171
bachelor's degrees 74
bacteria 104
Bacteriology 192
baggers 84
bags 85
Bailey, Billy 154
Bailey, Michael 154
Bailiff 171
Bainbridge (OH) 11, 32, 66, 81, 127, 128, 137, 159, 166, 172, 173, 174, 184
Bainbridge Branch Library 174
Bainbridge Community Church 50
Bainbridge Community United Church of Christ 51

Bainbridge Library 173, 174
Bakers Dozen Plus 94
baking 111
Baldwin 50
Baldwin, Sanford 81
balloon shop 131
ballroom 126, 159
Baltimore & Ohio Railroad (B&O) 108, 116, 120, 149; Station 161
band 93, 148
bandstand 148, 170
bank/s 90, 135, 137, 143
Bank One 19, 126
banquet 167
Baptist Church 56
Baptists 45
barbells 43
Barber, Robert, Rev. 43
barn raising 87
Barnes' Corners 28
Barnes, Bill 130
Barnes, Moses 35
Barnum, Bert 135
barrels 100, 135
Bartlett Family 25
Bartlett, Anson 35
baseball 146, 149; diamonds 144, 154; game 122
basket factory/ies 130, 139
bass 146
Bass Lake Development 159
Batavia 23
batch 106; plant 138
battery 98
Battle of Lake Champlain 35
Baumgartner, Emma 88
Beach, Carrie 34
Beales, A.C. 98
beams 129
beard 53, 109
bearing 132
Beaux and Belles 155
Becket, MA 32
Bedford (OH) 25
beds 163
Beech, George Washington 25
Beech, Maude 25, 135
Beech, Mildred 62
"Before I go out on the road" 178
Behm, Alton, Dr. 164
Belchertown, MA 32
belfrey 52
Belgians 82
bell/s 52, 115, 165; church 43, 45
Bell Road 108, 121, 146
Bell Vernon Creamery 122
Belsom, Jack E., Rev. 51
belt 87, 100
Benjamin, Asher 42
Benner, Bessie 71
Benton, Zadock, Jr. 52
Berkshire 60, 185, 192; High School 62, 94; School District 62, 185
Berkshire Hills Country Club 146
Berkshires 101
Berkshire, MA 32
Bessie Benner Metzenbaum Center; Foundation 71
Best Preserve, W.C. 16
Best Sand 117
Best, Walter 117
Bican, John, Mrs. 89
Bicentennial of the Constitution Committee 182
bicentennials 145
Bickle, Harry 180
Bickle, Henry 175, 180
Bicycle Step Ladder Company 135
Big Creek Park 16, 18
Big Wheel Plaza 128
Bigelow, Billy 170
Bingo 49
Binnig, Catharine 112
Binnig, George 112
birds 12
birth records 179
biscuits 84
Bishop 53
Blackmarr office building 181
blacksmith/s 128, 137, 160
Blandford, MA 32
blanket 115
bleach 105
blind 146, 150
blood 171; pressure 169
bloodmobile 171
Blue Spruce 90
Boak, Caroline E. 173
Board of Education 60
Board of Public Affairs 163
boating 15
Bode, Hugh, Father 47
Boehnlein, Charles 62
Bohemian 151
boiled down 104
boiling 100, 112
Bolton, Frances P., Honorable 160
bond issue 68
bond levy 174

Bond, Solomon, Dr. 25
Bondstown 25
Bondstown Logging Society 25
bones 24
bonnet 54
bookmobile 172
books 173
Booth, David 155
Booth, Ruth 155
boots 135
Boston 30
Bostwick, R.L. 137
Bottger, Marian 7, 28, 45, 46, 64, 108
bottle caps 141
boundaries 68
Bowden, Craig 14
Bower House 126
box 110; factories 127
Boy Scout/s 164, 182; Council 153
Bradley, Bildad 35
Brakeman, George 126
brass 137
Braunlich, Pat 173
bread 84, 87, 136
breakfast 109
Breunig, Rudy 15
Briar Hill 38, 171; Cemetery 38, 48; Church 48
brick 32, 181; making 127; mansion 175
bridge/s 6, 117
brine 19
bronze medal 104
Brooklyn United Church 50
Brooks, Peter Chardon 33, 52
Brown, Polly 32
Brown, William 35
Brown, William S., Rev. 44, 56
Brownie Troop 168
Brownlee, Hugh, Rev. 56
Bruce Brothers 131
Bruce, Williard 131
bucket/s 98, 100, 102, 103, 104
buckeye (tree) 101, 167
Buckeye Band 123
buckthorn sumac (tree) 102
Buffalo (NY) 25, 26
buggy/ies 77, 125
building/s 164, 165, 172; supply 138
bullet 59
bullfrog 97
Bullick, Alice 7
Bullick, William 7
bundle pitchers 84
Bundus, Sara 171
Bundy, Charles 181
Bundy, Elisha 27
Bundysburg 27
Burcaw, Lawrence, Rev. 49
Burg 25
Burkholder, Dan D., Jr. 53
Burlington 30
Burnett House 126
Burns, Helen 172
Burr, Edna 66; Hal 183
Burrows Road 67
Burton (OH) 16, 22, 25, 29, 30, 36, 43, 60, 62, 67, 68, 71, 77, 78, 84, 87, 89, 91, 92, 94, 97, 100, 108, 109, 112, 115, 116, 122, 123, 135, 145, 146, 152, 154, 158, 159, 166, 170, 172, 177, 178, 180, 184, 192
Burton, Camp 63, 146
Burton Century Village 154
Burton Chamber of Commerce 100
Burton Congregational Church 41
Burton Drug Company 7
Burton Fair 148
Burton Fairgrounds 91
Burton High School 62, 192
Burton Hotel 180
Burton Lakes 168
Burton Museum 172
Burton Police Department 173
Burton Public Library 74, 173, 192; Friends 158
Burton Rubber Processing 128
Burton Telephone Company 177
Burton Township 63
Burton Village 163, 173, 184
Burton Volunteer Fire Department 14, 166
Burton, Clifford, Sr. 84
Burton, Mae 50
Burton-Windsor Road 53
Burzanko, Jim 165
Burzanko, Sandy 165
bush 98
Bushman, Jane 7, 67, 117, 183
business/es 78, 127, 135, 144; development 117
Business and Professional Women's Club 164, 168
Butcher, Grace 178
Butt, Michael 18
butter 88; fat 86; milk 88
Butternut Road 63, 165
Byler, Crist U. 53
Byler, Dan A. 53
Byler, Ervin R. 53
Byler, Susan 171
Byler, Uria R. 53
Byler, William W. 53

C

cabin/s 32, 146, 147; log cabin 32, 33
cabinet maker 192
cable television 178
Cablevision 178
caboose 161
cafeteria 151
cake/s 55, 109; decorating 158
calendars 45
Calfee, Nancy 7, 31
California 179
camp/s 22, 63, 106, 146, 150
Campfire Girls 182
campgrounds 146
camping 15, 146, 147
campus 74
can/s 110
Canada 132
Canadian stations 178
canal 116
Cancer Fund Drive 164
candy making 109
cane spile 102
Canfield, Norman 33, 126
canning 107
Cannonball 155
canoe trips 146
Canton (OH) 30, 108, 161
canvas 84, 113
Cape Cod Dining Room 159
car 158
carded 133
Cardiac Club 175
Cardinal 61, 185; High School 63, 142; Middle School 60; School District 63, 185
cardio-pulmonary resuscitation 142, 171
Carlburg, Virginia 7, 179, 183, 185
Carlisle Corporation 139
Carlson, A. B. 112
Carlson, Arthur 100
Carnegie Library 174
Carousel 65, 170
carpenter 192
carpeting 133
Carr, Elizabeth 64
Carr, Julia 63
Carroll, Holly 174
cars 122, 125, 136
Carson, Steve 150
cart 92
Carter, Anthony 33
Carter, Ellen 31
Carter, Nancy 33
Carver, Laura (Clough) 32
Carver, Salmon 32
Carver, Solomon 32
Carver, Beverly 111
Case Western Reserve University 192
Casimatis, Peter 150
Cassel, Jean 50
cat 168
Cathedral Latin 72
Catholic Schools 60
Catholic Services Bureau 164
Catholics 47, 73
Cavanagh, Ignatius 112
caves 12
Caves Road 48, 130, 148, 178
CEI 95
celebration/s 17, 151, 158, 165, 170
cell 165
cement 123
cemetery/ies; 37, 38, 53, 81, 100; associations 164
census 184
Census Bureau 184
centennial/s 145, 165
Center for Human Services 164
Center schoolhouse 42
Center Street 52, 137, 143
Central Europe 78
century 183
Century Fair 92
Century Home 159
Century Village 36, 84, 152, 154, 159, 160, 161
Chadwick, Sally 34
Chagrin Falls (OH) 21, 69; Fair 148; Line 108, 121, 122
Chagrin Falls Park 168
Chagrin River 12, 13, 117
Chagrin Valley Athletic Club 159
Chagrin Valley Times 178
chair lift 74, 151
chalet 151
Chamber of Commerce 137, 169
Chamberlain, Joseph 32
Chamberlain, A.B.C. 77
Chamberlains Eye and Skin ointment 25
Chamberlin, A.B.C. 24
Chamberlin, Alonzo Burton Chauncy 24
Chamberlin, Amy 24
Chamberlin, Anney 24
Chamberlin, Dimas (Rowley) 25
Chamberlin, Dolly 24
Chamberlin, Elsie 24
Chamberlin, Ethel 24
Chamberlin, Forest 24
Chamberlin, George Leo 24

Chamberlin, Inez 24
Chamberlin, Louise 24
Chamberlin, Marion 24
Chamberlin, Martha (Winchell) 24
Chamberlin, Nelson 24
Chamberlin, Nelson H. 25
Chamberlin, Orlando 24
Chamberlin, Pete 24
Chamberlin, Ralph 24
Chamberlin, Rowena Belle (Strate) 24
Chamberlin, Roy 24
Chamberlin, William C. 24
Chamberlin/Chamberlain Family 24
Champion, OH 117
Chandler and Rudd 108
chapel 148
Chapman, G. L. (Shoe Store) 135
Chapman, Mike 141
Chapman, Ray 141
Chardon (OH) 12, 13, 16, 18, 25, 30, 32, 33, 47, 51, 60, 62, 64, 73, 74, 78, 91, 100, 101, 103, 115, 116, 117, 124, 126, 128, 135, 137, 143, 145, 149, 150, 159, 164, 165, 166, 167, 170, 171, 172, 175, 177, 178, 179, 180, 183, 184, 185, 192
Chardon Area Chamber of Commerce 137
Chardon Assembly of God 51, 52
Chardon Avenue 65, 73
Chardon Clothing Company 143
Chardon Development Company 137
Chardon Driving Association 149
Chardon High School 64, 65; School District 64
Chardon Historical Preservation Society 64
Chardon House Hotel 126
Chardon Kiwanis Club 101
Chardon Lakes 159
Chardon Lakes Golf 146; Course 159
Chardon Library 34, 174, 179, 192
Chardon Macaroni Company 135
Chardon Maple Festival 112
Chardon Metal Products 137
Chardon Methodist Church 52
Chardon Middle School 33
Chardon Municipal Court 163, 171
Chardon Plaza 128
Chardon Police Department 168
Chardon Preservation Society 64, 178
Chardon Public Schools 137
Chardon Rotary Club 192
Chardon Rubber 128
Chardon Rubber Company 135, 137
Chardon Savings Bank 19
Chardon Spectator 177
Chardon Square 51, 56
Chardon Square Association 170
Chardon Street Department 15
Chardon Telephone Company 177
Chardon Township 56
Chardon United Methodist Church 52, 192
Chardon Village 13, 34, 64, 163, 184; Cemetery 73
Charlie 17
Chatfield, Hale 178
cheese 127, 139; boxes 129
Cheese House 83, 139
cheesemaker 139
Chemical Dependency Unit 175
Cheney, Azro M. 93
Cherry Street 164
Chester (MA) 23
Chester (OH) 11, 23, 69, 148, 166, 184
Chester Branch Library 174
Chester Historical Park 178
Chester Township 57; Fire Department 166
Chester X (Cross) Roads 148
Chesterland (OH) 23, 56, 69, 128, 130, 148, 172, 174
Chesterland Baptist Church 56
Chesterland Brownie Troop 168
Chesterland Caves 148
Chesterland Historical Society 178
Chesterland News 178
Chesterland Shopping Center 128
chestnut, American (tree) 98
Chicago (IL) 104, 109, 135; Exposition 98
Chickagami, Camp 146, 153
chicken 87, 107
children 178
Childs, Jonas H. 32
Childs, Lydia (Kingsley) 32
Childs, Richard 7, 32, 38, 48, 83, 90
Childs-Taylor Chapter of the D.A.R. 182
Chillicothe (OH) 161
Chillicothe Road 38, 115, 116, 137, 174
chimney 98; stick 32
chipmunk 97
choir 170
Chorman, Betty 172, 173
Christiansen Family 108
Christmas 170; Eve 47; trees 93
church/es 38-57, 137, 146, 166, 170, 192
Church Building Society 42
Church on the Green 47
Church Street 43
churn 88
cinnamon 89
Civic Improvement Society 173
Civil War 154, 159, 177
Clapp, Eliza 134

apsaddle, Bill 22
arendon, VT 30
laridon (OH) 12, 30, 31, 33, 35, 62, 64, 65, 77, 85, 91, 93, 95, 104, 150, 165, 166, 170, 171, 175, 184, 192
laridon Antiques 131
laridon Center 41, 44, 131, 177; Cemetery 100
laridon Pond 12
laridon Town Hall 37, 95
laridon-Troy Road 42, 131
lark, Elizabeth 41
lark, Robert W. 163
ay 32, 97
lay Street 53
leaveland, Moses 21
leland, Mary 173
erk/s 163, 165, 172, 185
lerk's office 165
lerk-Treasurer 172
leveland (OH) 83, 108, 111, 116, 122, 141, 148, 151, 177, 178, 179, 192; Council 164
leveland & Eastern Railway 116, 122; Station 123
leveland Electric Illuminating Company 95
leveland Foundation 164
leveland Hopkins Airport 117
leveland Macaroni Company 135
leveland Museum of Natural History 24
leveland Soaring Society (gliders) 107
leveland Society for the Blind 150
leveland State University 30
leveland W. B. 147
leveland-Chardon line 122
lorox 100
osed ring 104
lough, Amasa 32
lough, Jare 32
lough, Laura 32
oves 89
ub/s 146, 158, 164, 170
lydesdale horses 17
o-educational 72
al 98, 120; handling 137
oats/es, Helen 25, 88
obblers 128
oder-Sestak, Jill 7, 154, 182
oeducational 70
ole, Hiram 28
ollector's item 155
ollier, Virgil 158
ollura, Mildred 171
olumbus (OH) 135
olumbus, Christopher 104
ombine 85
ombs 141
ommendation 93
ommercial 128, 143; applications 142
ommissioners 117, 163, 165, 168
ommissioners 185
ommittee of Preserve Our Community 95
ommon Pleas Court 165, 171; Judge 171
ommunity 164, 167, 169, 172, 174
ommunity Development Department 168
ompass 115
omputer/s 74, 164
onant's 98
oncentrate 106
oncord (Twp., Lake County, OH) 25, 35
oncrete 138
ongregational Church 40, 46; Burton 41; First of Claridon 41, 42, 192; Society 43
ongregationalist/s 44, 177
ongress 163
ongressional District 163
ongresswoman 160
ONICAL 137
onneaut River 116
onnecticut 21, 25, 33, 42, 74, 85, 137, 147
onnecticut Land Company 21
onnectors 105, 141
onscientious objectors 40
onservation 78
onsolidation 68
ontest 101
ontinental Army 182
ontract 179
ontractor 141, 169
onverse House 136
ook House 22
ook, Doris 10, 22, 25, 28, 41, 55, 57, 60, 62, 63, 64, 66, 70, 74, 111, 124, 142, 155, 158, 169, 171, 172, 174
ook, Marimon 74
oon 97
ooperative Extension Service 7
opper 106, 137, 138
orbus, Lawrence J. 172, 174
orliss, C. G. 29
orn 84, 87, 90, 94, 98; knife 84; planter; seed 87
orn Pancake Mix 113
ornish, Don 173
ornish, Donald 172
ornstalks 60
oroner 185
orrigan, Betsy 172
ottage industries 128
ottage Pottery 152, 192

cottages 151
council/s 116, 163, 168
Council President 168
counselor 167
County Airport Development Program 117
County Line Road 14
county seat 33, 177
Covenant 40
Cowles, Asa 30, 42
Cowles, Pem, Dr. 182
cows 84, 86
coyotes 85
CPR 142, 171
crafts 152
Cragg, Doris (Millard) 53, 54, 83, 86, 143
Cragg, Perry 53, 54, 83, 84, 86, 143
Crandall, Homer 67
crappie 146
Cravens, John 185
Crazy Wheels 73
cream 88, 111
criminal 163
crisis 167; intervention 164
Crittenden Drug Store 173
crocks 88
Cromwell, W. H. 181
crops 19, 90
Cross, Elmer 173
Crossroads Country Store 161
Crowe, Mary 173
Crownvetch 90
culinary skills 55
Cullum, Kathleen "Kay" 155
Cunningham, Pauline 50
cupola 165
Cuyahoga 22; River 12, 21, 23, 116
Cuyahoga County (OH) 20, 21, 69, 128, 164, 178; Public Library 192
Czecho-Slovak people 151
Czechoslovakia 151

D

D.A.R. 164, 182
Dacklewicz, Stan 15
dam 153
Damon 130
Dana's Institute 148
Daniels, Ruth 174
Daughters of the American Revolution 164, 182
Dauler, George 154
Davies Can Company 110
Davis, Edna 163, 182, 185
day care 170
Day, Margaret 27
Days of Christmas Past 170
Dayton, Friend 29
deacon 53
dean 74
death records 179
Dedek, Vince 63
deer 146
Deerfield, NY 48
degree 106
DeGroft, Elsie 112
DeGroft, Glenn 112
deionization 142
Dell, Robert 170
demolition 179
DeMuth, Ann 155
Depression 132
descendants 78
design 141
desserts 87
Detroit (MI) 147
Detty, David E., Rev. 44
Detweiler, Dan A. 53
Detweiler, Rudy A. 53
Detweiler, Sam C. 53
Developmentally Handicapped 60
dials 106
Diedrich, Johanna 171
Dillon, Rodney, Jr. 7, 48
Dimmick, Alger 170
Dimmick, Ethel 170
Dimmick, Royal 35
dining 159
Disabilities, Developmental 71
disaster relief 171
Disraeli, Benjamin 145
distillery/ies 128, 147
district schools 62
districts 53
Dively, Jean 173
doctors 167
documents 160
Dog Sled Racing 152
dog/s 85, 150, 168
Dolezal, Raymond "Buck" 7, 136
dome 140
Domestic Hall 91
donations 161
Doolittle, Lottie 92
dormitories 151
Douglass, James 22
Dow, Charles, Mrs. 173
Downes, Randolph 183
draft horses 82
dramatics 65

dreams 94
dress 133; code 67; making 133
drill 98; press 88
drought 12
drugstore/s 7, 23, 27, 69, 125, 141, 173, 175, 181
drum 107
Dufur, Karen 101
Duramax, Inc. 132
Durham, Brian 159
Durham, Jim 159
Durkee Road 69
Dutton, Jessie 89

E

eagle 37
Eagles 164
ears 176
earth-moving equipment 124
earthquakes 12
East Branch 12, 117, 146
East Claridon 33, 44, 62, 177
East Elm Street 123
East High Street 123, 138
East Park Street 64
Eastern Star Lodge 164
Easy Street 43
Eckart, Dennis E., Congressman 93, 163
Eckhard, Henry 94
Eckles, Beebe 170
education 40, 184
Eggleston, Chauncey, Gen. 81
eggs 100
elder 98
elderberry 102
elderly 125, 165
election 60
electric 94; cord 141; traction 116
electrical supplies 138
electronic 138; industry 141
Elementary Supervisor 63
elevator 108
Elliot, Karen 172
Ellsworth, England 29
elm (tree) 136, 182
Elm Street 123
Ely, Hazel 50
emergency 168
Emmenthaler Valley (Switz.) 139
employment 142
encampment 159
energy 19
engineer 84, 116, 124, 188; ing 78, 106, 137
England 21
English 59, 178
Ensign, H. N. 104
Ensign, James 104
Ensign, Maria 31
entertainment 155
enumerator 184
environment 94
Episcopal Church 56, 57
equipment 166
Erie 178; Indians 21; Lake 12, 20, 21, 90, 116; Railroad 116
Ernst, Walter 67
erosion control 78
Ervin, Ann 171
estate 175
Evangelical and Reformed Churches 40
Evangelism Sunday 57
Evans, Albert, Dr. 138, 185
Evans, Carol 73
Evans, Upshur, Mrs. 16
evaporation 97, 98
evaporator/s 98, 100, 104, 106
Exceen, Maria 134
Exchange Hotel 180
Excommunication 40
execution 33
Executive Director 164
extinguishing service 169
extruded 137; rubber 139
Eye and Skin ointment 25
Eykyn, Mary 174

F

factory 35, 130, 135, 137
Fagerburg, Joanne 74
fair 91, 92; Great Geauga County 40, 60, 78, 85, 145; band 93; Board 122
fairgrounds 91, 122, 170, 182
Fairmount Road 14, 38, 90
Fairport (OH) 25; Harbor 120
Falcon Aviation 117
Fantasy, A 97
Farley, Hilton 112
farm/s 87, 90, 98, 146, 151; implements 85; machinery 91
farmer/s 29, 84, 85, 90, 91
farming 77, 78
fellowship 164, 167, 178
felony 163
felt 107
Feltes, Catherine 50
fences 127, 139

Ferris (Ave.) 73
Ferris, Alice 172; Chalmer 183
Ferris, Duane 16; Howard 183
Ferry, Alice 27
fertilizer 87
festival/s 40, 43, 60, 72, 73, 88, 100, 101, 106, 108, 110, 111, 141, 145, 156
Festival Parade 101
festive 155
fibers 84
fiction 178
FIDDLER ON THE ROOF 65
Fiegle, Frank 109
field trips 74
Fifth Avenue 137
files 164
filter 107
Finch, Ernest 148
Fine Arts Show 170
Finley, John 28
fire/s 43, 89, 97, 98, 108, 126, 159, 161, 165; fire 166, 169, 177, 179, 180, 181; chief 169; chief's association 166; department/s 136, 163, 166; prevention 78, 166; station 169
Fire Lands (OH) 20
Firebird Aviation 117
fireplace 165
fireworks 115
first aid 171
First Congregational Church of Claridon 41, 42
First Congregational Church of Claridon 170, 192
First County Bank 137
First Disciple Church 47
First National Bank of Burton 135
First United Methodist Church 49
First United Methodist Church of East Claridon 44
Fischer, Candy 168
fish 12, 87
Fisher, Elizabeth "Lee" 155
Fisher John 59
fishing 15, 84, 146, 147
Fitness Center 159
Flahaven, Michael 117
flax 84
flood protection 78
floor, puncheon 32
flooring 139
Flooring Products Division 132
flour 135
flower 80; arranging 158; girl 150; seedlings 93
Flowering Tree Packet 90
Floyd, NY 48
flue 106
flywheel 84
FM 178
food 78, 115; dog and cat 168
Food Service 66
Ford, Easter 145
Ford, H. H. 91
Ford, Henry Hine, Col. 145
Ford, John 145
Ford, Richard 168
Ford, Robert 16
Ford, Robert B., Judge 171
Ford, Seabury 178
Forestry, Division of 90
forests 11, 78, 115
Fourth of July celebration 151
Fowler's/Fowlers Mill/s 124, 160; Christian Church 45; Golf Course 146; Road 117
Fowler, Jim 52
Fox, Arletta 34
Fox, G. B. 92
Fox, Lottie (Doolittle) 92
Fox, Marilyn 172
Fox, Maurice 22, 109
Frank, Peter 159
Frank, Skip 151
Franks, Elmer 112
Franks, Esther 112
Fraternal Orders 164
Free Democrat 177
Free Soil Party 177
freedom 40, 116
French, Avery Marell 27
French, Avery Marvin 27
French, Bessie 27
French, Charles 27
French, Charles Leroy 27
French, Crosby 27
French, Emma 27
French, Emma Ella (Wolfe) 27
French, Hannah 27
French, John 174
French, Lorena Mae 27
French, Margaret (Day) 27
French, William 7, 27
Frenchie, Richard J. 175
freshet 80
Friendly Visitor 171
Friends of the Bainbridge Library 173
Friends of the Burton Library 158
Frohring Foundation 22
Frohring, Gertrude, Mrs. 22
Frohring, R. L. 141
fruit 28, 138
Fugman, Jean 34

Fuller, Cynthia 81
Fuller, James 81
Fuller, Laura 192
Fuller, R. Buckminster 140
fun 145
fund raising 55, 164
fundraiser/s 70, 150
funds 164, 168
furniture 132

G

G.A.R. Highway (Federal Route 6) 116, 124
Gall, Tony 163, 185
gallon 100
galvanizing 98
game/s 146
Game Protector 11
garden/s 151; clubs 164
Garfield Heights (OH) 22
Garfield, James A. 46, 145
Garrettsville (OH) 27
gas 19, 98; heater 106; wells 12, 19; natural 43
gaskets 132, 137
Gates Mill stop 148
Gates Mills (OH) 70
gauges 100
Gay Nineties 170
gears 141
Geauga Air Services 117
Geauga Assisted Living 171
Geauga Board of Realtors 154
Geauga Cannonball 155
Geauga Christian School 70
Geauga Co-operative Ministry 40, 41, 42, 45, 51
Geauga Community Hospital 163, 172
Geauga Community Mental Health Board 164
Geauga County 20, 21, 74
Geauga County Agricultural and Manufacturing Society 91
Geauga County Airport 117, 125
Geauga County Board of Education 61, 178
Geauga County Board of Education, Annual Report 60
Geauga County Centennial Celebration 165
Geauga County Clerk of Courts 185
Geauga County Coins and Jewelry 143
Geauga County commissioners 16, 117, 163
Geauga County Court House 25, 165, 182
Geauga County Court of Appeals 171
Geauga County Court of Common Pleas 163
Geauga County Department of Human Services 170; (welfare) 71
Geauga County Department on Aging 170
Geauga County engineer 116
Geauga County Firemen's Association 166
Geauga County Genealogical Society 34, 179, 192
Geauga County Grand Jury 163
Geauga County Granges 77
Geauga County Highway Department 124
Geauga County Historical Society 7, 22, 47, 61, 74, 81, 84, 87, 88, 89, 98, 145, 155, 160, 172, 178
Geauga County Home 30, 175
Geauga County Humane Society 168
Geauga County Maple Festival 111
Geauga County Medical Association 167
Geauga County Mental Health Association 164
Geauga County National Bank 137
Geauga County Park District 12, 154
Geauga County Planning Commission 127, 183, 184
Geauga County Public Library 7, 164, 172, 173, 174, 175, 179, 184, 192
Geauga County Recorder 174
Geauga County Retired Teachers Association 66
Geauga County Sanitary Engineer's Department 37
Geauga County Sheriff 164
Geauga County YMCA 146
Geauga Democrat 177
Geauga Family Services 164
Geauga Freeman 177
Geauga Gazette 177
Geauga Hospital 39, 175
Geauga House 126
Geauga Industries 139
Geauga Lake 12, 146, 180; Park 146
Geauga Leader 177
Geauga Livestock Commission 143
Geauga Lyric Theater Guild 170
Geauga News 177
Geauga Oral History Project 25
Geauga Park District 16, 17, 18, 146
Geauga Preservation Society 94, 95
Geauga Record 177
Geauga Republican 98, 119, 177
Geauga Republican and Whig 177
Geauga Republican-Record 177
Geauga Savings Bank 143
Geauga Seminary 69
Geauga Times Leader 7, 78, 177, 178
Geauga Transit 125
Geauga West Library 174
Geauga, Cleveland & Mahoning Valley Railway 116
Geauga-Trumbull Schools 59
GEAUGANSPEAK 23, 71, 192

Geaugrapher 90
geese 17
Gehri, Gene 163
Genealogical; Research 179; Society 34, 179, 192
General Signal Corporation 137
general store/s 127, 128, 130, 181
genetic engineering 78
Geneva, NY 30
geodesic dome 140
geography 12, 60
geraniums 93
Gerlach, Jay 81
German 59
Germany 78
Gharky, Pleman 92
Gibbs, Myron 169
Gierlach, Annette 158
gift shop 131
Gifted and Talented programs 60
Gilbert, William 181
Giles Lake 146
Giles Pond 12
Gillen, Frank 155
ginger 89
Gingerich, Andy A. 53
Gingerich, Crist A. 53
Gingerich, Phil 17
Gingerich, William A. 53
Girdled Road 116
Girl Scouting 168
Girl Scouts 164
glacier 147
glass plate/s negatives 179, 183
Glasscock Oscar 14
Glenn Machine and Service Corporation 141
Glenn, John 163
Glenn, Kim 7, 149, 179
gliders 117
GO 73
golf 146, 147, 158; courses 151
Gonczy, Jane Kay 41
Good News 178
Goodrich, Wesley 149
Goodwin, Clinton 98
Goodwin, Homer 145
Goodyear Tire Dealer Magazine 73
Goold, Lavinia 40
Goose Pond 37
Gorman, Hannah 33
Gorman, Lewis 33
Gorris, Wendy 73
government 163, 177; federal 115
gowns 133
graduation 60
grain 79, 84, 85, 94, 128
granary 84
Grand Army of the Republic 116
Grand Jury 163
Grand River 12, 25, 26, 116; presbytery 43
grandparents 60
grandstand 91
Grandview Inn and Golf Club 146
Grangers 77
Granges 77, 164
grant 168; federal 168
Grant Street 34
Grant, Arletta (Fox) 34
Grant, Betsy (Marshall) 34
Grant, Carrie (Beach) 34
Grant, Charles 34
Grant, Chicken 34
Grant, Dick 34
Grant, Edward 34
Grant, Glen 34
Grant, Grace Armena (Alderman) 34
Grant, John 34
Grant, Leonard, Jr. 34
Grant, Leonard, Sr. 34
Grant, Lloyd W. 34
Grant, Mabeletta 34
Grant, Minnie 34
Grant, Myrtle 34
Grant, Noma A. (Trask) 34
Grant, Orie 34
Grant, Roy Robert 34
Grant, U.S., General 154
Grant, William 7, 34
gravel 6, 124
gravestones 32
graze 85
Great Lakes Mall 128
Green, Fred 171; Hal 183
Green, Harlan Page 108
Green, Robert 24
Green, Wallace 67
Greening of America 154
Griddle Cake Pancake Mix 113
Grieg, Andy 164
Grieshaber, Paul 125
Griffith, Steve 180
grinding wheel 85
gristmill/s 70, 80, 127, 147
grocery 181
Grosvenor woods 100
Grosvenor, Belle 112
Grosvenor, Jeannette "Teeter" 23, 60, 62, 179, 183, 192
Grosvenor, John Flavel 97

Grosvenor, June 62
Grosvenor, Laura (Fuller) 192
Grosvenor, Nathan 192
Grosvenor, R. C. 85
Grosvenor, Ralph 62
groundbreaking 142
Grover, Melvin 62
Guernseys 86
Guiness Book of Records 110
Gumpper, Mary Fran 173
Guren, Peter 180
Guys and Dolls 65
gymnasium 67
gymnasts 151

H

Haas, Becky 73
Hagens, Jesse 170
Hladene, Janet 67
Hale Farm (Jonathon) 97
Half a Man 94
hall 91
Hambden (OH) 24, 25, 33, 34, 35, 64, 65, 77, 141, 166, 184, 192
Hambden Building Products 141
Hambden Congregational Church 141
Hambden Elementary School 64
Hambden Orchard 146
Hambden Township Park 154
Hammond, Horace 180
Hampden 25
handicapped 43, 60, 125, 146, 150
handwriting 183
hangar 117
hanging 33
hardware 100, 143
hardwood 127
Harpers Ferry 28
Harrington Square Mall 128
Harrington, Terry 172
Harris, Bill 151
Hartland 85
Harvan, Nate 22
Harvey 65
hat 53
Haueter, Russell 170
Hausmann, Harold 62
Hausmann, Loretta 62, 164
Hausmann, Matilda 62
Hausmann-Holmes Scholarship 40
Hawken Upper School 70
Hawken, James A. 70
Hawley, MA 29
hay 85, 94; loader 85
Haynes, Sharon 65, 154, 170
hazard 91
Head, Charles 173
healing 104
health 163; care; department 169
hearings 163
Heather Hill Nursing Home 171
Heiden, Catherine H. 185
Hein, Linda 66
Henry, Thompson Store 134
Henry, Charles E. 163
heritage 145, 167, 177, 179
heroes 167
Herrick Drive 174, 179
Herrick, — 179
Herrington, Doris 50
Herrington, Lloyd 7
hickory (tree) 98
Hickox Brick Museum 160
Hickox farm 98
Hidden Valley Golf Course 146
High Street 122, 123, 134, 173
Highbrook Lodge 146, 150
Highland Hotel 126, 167
Highway Garage 116
hiking trails 147
Hill, Ed 56
Hill, Henry 37, 98, 104
Hill, Mary 56
hills 94
Hiram College 178
Hiscox, Jerry 14
historian 136
Historical Collections of Ohio 115
historical society/ies 7, 22, 47, 61, 74, 81, 84, 87, 88, 89, 98, 145, 155, 160, 172, 178
history 154, 183, 192
History of Geauga and Lake Counties, Ohio 183
Hoard, Harrison 29
Hodges 129
Hoffman, Fred 70
Hofstetter, Edwin, Judge 171
Holbury, William, Mrs. 160
Hollenbeck Apartments 126
Hollenbeck, S. D. 126
hollow log 98
Holly Hill Nursing Home 171
Holmes County 77, 78
Holmes, Loretta Mae (Hausmann) 164, 166
Holstein cows 86
Holzheimer, David 173, 174
home 147

home economics 66
homecoming/s 68, 145
homemaker 89
homemaking 78
Ho-Mita Koda, Camp 146
hoops 103
Hornak, Ross 159
Hornak, Todd 159
horse/s 17, 81, 82, 84, 97, 98, 107, 126, 129, 167, 180; race park 149; show 158; drawn equipment 124; pulling 82
horsemen 92
Horton, Lee 168
hose/s 107, 137, 169
Hosford Hill 124
Hosford, Lynn H. 112
Hosmer, Ford 92
Hosmer, Henry L. 29
Hosmer, Hilda 109
hospital/s 30, 142, 163, 172, 175
Hossler, Mabel 62
Hostetler, Eli S. 53
hotel 126, 129, 167, 180, 181
house, brick 32
Hovey's Drug Store 175
Howard, Vernon 93
Howe, 115; Henry 183
Hubbard, Clarence 34
Hubbard, Florence 34
Hubbard, Grace Armena (Alderman) 34
Hult, Anna Jane 172
Human Service Agencies 164
human services 163, 175; Department of 170
Human Services Forum 166
humidity 88
Humiston, James 98
Humphrey, Luther, Rev. 33, 42
Hunt, Judy 85
Hunt, Lewis 28
hunting 15, 146
Hunting Valley Village 184
Huntington Bank 148
Huntington National Bank 135
Huntley Road 53
Huntsburg (OH) 12, 23, 28, 50, 62, 63, 77, 133, 134, 145, 178, 180, 184
Huntsburg Center 84
Huntsburg Congregational Church 43
Huntsburg Elementary School 67
Huntsburg Grange #1588 77
Huntsburg Miller-Amish Cemetery 53
Huntsburg South Amish Church 53
Huntsburg South District 53
Hurlburt, Rufus 42
Huron County 20
Husbandry, Patrons of 77
Hyde, Virginia 7, 22, 42, 85
hydraulic lines 137
Hymn of Promise 80
hypertension 169

I

I Can Cope 175
I.O.O.F. 71, 164; building 136
ice age 147
ice cream 59, 136
ice-skating rink 147
immigrate 151
imported foods 139
incineration systems 137
income 120
Independence Day 22
Inderlied, H. F. 163
Inderlied, H. F., Judge 171
indexed records 179
Indian/s 21, 22, 23, 25, 98, 102
industry/ies 120, 126-144, 169, 184
Info-Line/Volunteer Bureau 164, 166
information 164
injection molding machinery 141
ink 59; pails 132
inner tube 146
international Order of Odd Fellows 164
intersection 123
interurban/s 12, 91, 108, 116, 121, 122, 148
interurban electric traction 116
invented 137
Ireland 117
iron ore 120

J

Jackam, Chris 159
Jackam, John 159
Jackson Hardwood Lumber Company 139
Jackson, Art 139
Jackson, Donald C. "Mike" 139
Jackson, Ed 139
Jackson, Francis 139
Jacobs, Paul C. 172
jail 165
jam 59
Jamieson, Isabel 92
Janson, Cecelia 66
Janssen, Kenny 91
Japanese garden 24
Jefferson 47
Jeffersonian Democrat 177
Jerseys 86

sse, Helen 172
sse, Richard, Rev. 57
vnikar, Jane 33
hnson Rubber Company 128, 132, 139
hnson Store 173
hnson, Fred 158
hnson, Harriet Ely 172, 174
hnson, Joe 132
hnson, Jonathan 37
hnson, Joseph 23
hnson, Kathy 173
hnson, Mabel 50
hnson, Solomon, Sr. 107
hnson, Ture 90, 112
nes, Larry D., Dr. 74
rdon, Julie 170
urnal of Emily Nash 113
yce, David P. 185
dge/s 163, 171
nior Choir Festival 40, 43
stice 165

K

assinger, Tim 173, 174
auffman, JoAnn 171
auffman, Loma 171
aye, Jennie 111
eener, Jefferson W., Jr. 137
elleher, Vince 173
ellogg schoolhouse 42
ellogg, Frank 62
ellogg, June (Grosvenor) 62, 85
enny, Rita 66
enston 185; High School 66; School District 185
ent (OH) 74, 108
ent State University 74; Geauga Campus 23, 64, 71, 178, 192
ent, Matt 64
entstown 32
ershner, Stephen 172
ettle/s 89, 98 107, 113
ewley, Jim 142
id hack 64
ids 161
ile Road 146
illeen, Dennis 136
iller whale 182
iln 139
impton, Thomas 29
inetico 142
ing, — 25
ing, Jabez, Mrs. 33
ing, Kevin 71
ing, Samuel 33
ingsley, Lydia 32
ingsville, TX 25
insman Road 116, 140, 141
irby, Aubrey E., Rev. 52
irtland 13
iwanis (Club) 164
iwanis Lake (OH) 168
leinfeld, Harold 62
leinfeld, Julius 85
napp, Dorothy (Parsons) 7, 150, 179
nife 85, 107, 110; chicken caller 107
nights of Columbus 164
nights of Pythias 164; Hall 138
nitting lessons 55
orey, Neil 14, 71, 150, 171
ozak, Allison 111
oziol, Joseph 170
KraftMaid Cabinetry, Inc. 142
ristoff, Wendy 70
ronk, Kenneth 93

L

labels 110
Labor Day 148, 152
laboratories 141, 142
Ladd, Elizabeth (Clark) 41
Ladd, T. Dwight 39, 41, 93, 101
LaDue, 12; Reservoir 15, 146
LaDue, Wendell Richard 15
Ladyzhensky, Leroy 22
lake/s 12, 20, 21, 29, 90, 116, 128, 146, 147, 153, 168
Lake Aquilla 12, 146
Lake Avenue 144
Lake County (OH) 74, 116, 128, 138, 165
Lake County News-Herald 60
lake effect 12
Lake Erie Girl Scout Council 183
Lake Lucerne 12
Lake Punderson 29
Lake-Geauga Center for Alcoholism 164
Lakeland Community College 168
Lakewood 22
Lamaze/Pre-Natal Classes 175
land 94
Landi, Al 158
landmarks 81
Lang, Albert 17
Lang, Donna 7, 166
Language Arts 63
lantern 113
Laro, Deena 168
Lavrich, Frank G. 163

law enforcement 163, 164
Lawrence, Philinda B. 48
laws 19
lawyer 55
leadership 78
Leagan, Gloria Jean 183
League of Women Voters 16, 172
Leaman, Wade 80
Learn, Frank 71
lecturer 178
Ledgemont 60, 185; High School 172, 181; Local School District 67, 185
ledger 184
ledges 6, 12
legal fees 95
Legend Lake Golf Club 146
legislature 163
Lehmann, Glenda 155
leisure 145
Lennon, Patrick 14
Lenten Series 40
Leonard, F. M. 12
Let's Explore Ohio 45
levy 16, 60
librarian 174
Library Science 192
library/ies 7, 74, 158, 160, 163, 164, 172, 173, 174, 175, 184, 192; board 174
lifestyle 78
Lillibridge, Missy 158
Linch, Judg 28
Lincoln, (Abraham), President 163, 178
Linden, Milton 62
Linden, Vivian 62
line verse 63
linseed oil 84
linsey-woolsey 84, 85
Linton, Donald 16
liquid 100
liquors, spirituous 29
Litke, Howard 62
Litke, Lottie 62
Little Mountain 12
Lockert, Mildred 66
Lodge Pond 17
log/s 98, 100; building 165; cabin 108, 109, 126
Long, Karl 147
loom 133
Lorain County (OH) 20
lounge 151
Loveland Family 67
Luckay, Bill "Lucky" 155
Luckay, William 170
lumbers 100
Lybarger, Don 159

M

macaroni 135; factory 137
Maccabees 164
Mace, Dave 181
machine 141
Mack, Dawn 154
MacMurray, Marie 125
Madison Road 53, 116
Mahoning County (OH) 138
Maiden, Geneva 172
mail carrier/s 138, 180
Main Street 51, 52, 62, 120, 123, 126, 138, 165, 173
Main Street 179, 180, 183
Majka, Bob 135
Makowski, Richard J. 185
Malensek, Christine 62
Malensek, Louis 62
Malensek, Stanley 62
Malensek, Ursula 62
Mall 111, 128
Malzer, Edward, Rev. 45
Malzer, Shirley, Rev. 45
management 74
manager 159
manager 113
Manor House 147
mansion 147
manufacturing 132
manure 55
manuscripts 160
map 61
maple/s 98, 101, 111; camp 106; cream 112; hard 98; leaves 110; sugar 110; syrup 96-113, 127; tree 97, 102
Maple Avenue 65
Maple Elementary School 65, 74
Maple Festival 60, 100, 108, 110, 145
Maple Hill Nursing Home 171
Maple Stir 112
Maple Sugar Center of the World 101
Maple Syrup Hall of Fame 112
Marek, Alice 62
Marek, Blanche 62
Marek, Joseph 62
Marie, the Seeing Eye dog 150
Marietta (OH) 180
Marietta, Nancy 172
marine 132
marital status 184
Maroush, Anne 173
Marriage Encounter United Methodist 192

marriage records 179
Marshall, Betsy 34
Marshall, Polly (Rider) 34
Marshall, Tina 64
Marty, NY 48
Maryland 28
Masonic Lodge 164
Massachusetts 22, 23, 25, 32, 33, 178
Mast, Eli J. 53
Mast, John J. 53
Mast, Lester J. 53
Mast, William J. 53
mastodon 24, 35
materialism 40
Mather 16
Matlock Tim 173
Mayfield Road 30, 33, 36, 42, 43, 53, 93, 116, 131, 166, 174, 178
mayor 163, 168
McConoughey, David 32
McCullough, Robert 17
McDonough 30, 35
McGuffy readers 59, 60, 61
McIntosh, Kenneth 16
McKinney, Charles E., Jr. 168
McLaughlin, Maria 89
McLaughlin, Terry 172
McLean, Margaret 181
McNaughton, Ellen (Chamberlin) 24
McNaughton, Lydia 7, 25
McNaughton, Ralph 24
McNish, Howard 112
McNish, Paul 112
meal 87
measurement 97
meat 87
medicine 167; wagon 141
Medina County (OH) 20
Meek, Mindy 110
membership 159
memorial 160
Memorial Day 72
Men's and Ministers' Dinner 40
Mennonite/s 40, 78, 171
mental health 163, 164
Mental Retardation 71
Mentor (OH) 23, 128
Mentor Road 124
Merritt, Helen 173
Merritt, Stanlae 92, 124, 180
Merryfield, Hope 138
Merryfield, Marten, Jr. 138
Merryfield, Marten, Mrs. 138
Merryfield, Marten, Sr. 138
Mesopotamia (OH) 61, 116, 171
Mesopotamia Road 26
Messenger (Middlefield) 178
Messenger, Howard 112
metal/s 102; recovery 142
Metals Park 140
meters 100
Methodist/s 51, 52, 177, 192; Association 45; Conference 51; preacher 25
Methodist Church 43, 51; First United 49; First United of East Claridon 44; Middlefield United 50; Middlefield Wesleyan 49; Thompson United 46
Methodist Episcopal 49
Metzenbaum Center 71; School 71
Metzenbaum, Bessie Benner 71
Metzenbaum, Howard 163
Meyer Center, Donald W. 18
Meyer, Don 16
Meyer, George 18
Meyer, Jim 18
Meyer, Mary Lou 18
Michigan 90
Michigan Bell 13
Middlefield (OH) 10, 17, 23, 24, 27, 37, 49, 60, 61, 63, 69, 77, 78, 82, 85, 95, 107, 115, 116, 117, 119, 120, 122, 123, 128, 132, 133, 134, 138, 139, 141, 142, 143, 144, 145, 156, 161, 169, 170, 171, 172, 178, 184
Middlefield Chamber of Commerce 169
Middlefield Cheese House 83, 139
Middlefield Electric Company 138
Middlefield Junior High School 173
Middlefield Library 173
Middlefield Messenger 177
Middlefield Municipal Center 119
Middlefield North District 53
Middlefield Swiss Cheese Co-op 139
Middlefield Times 177
Middlefield United Methodist Church 50
Middlefield Village 63, 163, 184
Middlefield Wesleyan Methodist 49
Mikado 170
military 137
milk 35, 86, 139
milking stools 59
Millard, Doris 53, 54
mill/s 80, 81, 98, 100, 115, 127, 129, 133
miller's knot 85
Miller, Albert G. 53
Miller, Allen A. C. 53
Miller, Andy 42
Miller, Carol 173
Miller, Chester D. 53
Miller, Dan E. 53

Miller, Dan J. B. 53
Miller, David 77, 78
Miller, Edna 71
Miller, Joe A. 53
Miller, Kenneth 41
Miller, Noah J. 53
Miller, Paul 173
Miller, Paul C., Jr. 132
Miller, Paul C., Sr. 132
Miller, Priscilla 171
Miller, Ray 142
Miller, Warren H. 25
Miller, William F. 132
Miller-Amish Cemetery 53
millinery 181
Mills (Neher & Mills) 130
millwork 139
Miner, Barbara 173
Miner, John, Dr. 13
Miner, Justice 23
Mineral Lake Park 144
miniature golf 146
ministers 53
minority outreach 172
Minterns Lunch and Ice Cream Stand 136
Miscko, Chris 168
mission 70
mixer, cement 123
mixes 113
Mlaker, Edith Lynn 33
Moffet, Marcus 44; Jim 183
molding 137, 141
molds 110
Montague, Betty J. 185
Montville (OH) 35, 67, 111, 130, 132, 161, 166, 167, 171, 184
Montville Church of Christ 44
Montville Elementary School 67
Montville United Methodist Church 44
Monumental Work 192
Moodie, Richard M. 142
Moran, James J., Father 73
Mordoff, Erma 65
Morgan, Bill 14
Mormino, Pam 168
Morning Star Coffeehouse 46
Morse, John Henry 133
Morton Cemetery 37
Mosenthal, Bobbie 174
Moss Lake 153
Moss, Narvie 80
Moster's Hardware 143
mothers' club 164
motto 78
Mount Union College 192
mower 85
Mowery, Carl 7, 181
mowing 84
MSI Print Shop 71
mud 98, 119
Mueller, James 158, 163, 185
Mueller, Sandra 59
mule-drawn equipment 124
mules 176
Mullet, Jake L. 53
Mullett, Chad 70
Multiple Sclerosis Society 125
MuMac Theatre 138
Mumford, Mabeletta (Grant) 34
Mumford, Otto 34
Municipal Court 163
Munson (OH) 11, 25, 30, 35, 64, 65, 69, 72, 117, 124, 166, 169, 171, 184
Munson Fire Department 166
Munson Grange #1549 77
Munson Town Hall 36, 160
Munson Township 74
murder 33
Murphey, Robert E., Rev. 38
museum 24, 38, 87, 139, 181; grounds 60
music 101; clubs 164
Music Street 139
musical 93
musicians 101
musket 28
muskrat 97
mustaches 53
My Three Angels 65
Myers, Jeff 161

N

Naiman, Deborah 61, 168
Nalman, Deborah 14
Nash Family 113
Nash, A. J. 129
Nash, Emily 22, 27, 28, 30, 33, 113
Nash, John 113
National Archives 35
National Endowment for the Humanities 178
National Grange of the Patrons of Husbandry 77
National High Blood Pressure Month 169
National Railway Historical Society 108
National Register of Historic Places 42
naturalist 16
Nautilus area 159
Nauvoo Road 143
Navy aircraft carrier 125

Neaves and Hodges 129
negatives 179, 183
Negroes 178
Neher and Mills 130
neighborhood 185; schools 62
Neiman, Deborah 161
New Beginnings 164
New France 21
New Hampshire 29
New Haven, CT 147
New York (City) 127
New York (State) 22, 24, 27, 29, 30, 35, 48
Newbury (OH) 22, 29, 35, 37, 49, 59, 71, 73, 116, 121, 129, 138, 139, 143, 146, 155, 166, 171, 178, 184, 185
Newbury Auto Parts 143
Newbury Box Factory 129
Newbury Center 129
Newbury Community Church 45
Newbury Cornet Band 148
Newbuy Grange 77
Newbury High School 68
Newbury Industries 141
Newbury, NH 29
Newbury Pharmacy 143
Newbury School 68; Auditorium 170; District 185
Newbury, VT 29
Newburyport, MA 29
Newcomb Road School 59
Newell, Lectrus J. 30
Newell, Lydia 141
Newell/Grosvenor farm 98
Newman, Paul 172
newspaper/s 177, 178, 180; office 74
Newton Falls 108
Nichols, Grant 148
Nokes, Jeff 125
North American continent 100
North Cheshire Street 91
North Hambden 34
North Street 73
Northup, Lucy 27
Northwest Territory 21
Notre Dame 60; Academy 72, 173; Cathedral Latin High School 72; Elementary School 72
Novak, Helen 88
Novelty (OH) 37, 48, 140, 158
nuclear power plants 137
nurse 169, 172
nursing home/s 171
nut trees 90
Nutricise 175
Nutt, David 48
Nutt, Philinda B. (Lawrence) 48
Nutt, Will 83

O

O'Connor, Kevin, Rev. 56
O'Meara, John R. 17
oats 83
occupation 184
Odd Fellow's Hall 71
office building 181
officials 163
Ohio 30, 37, 74, 78, 110, 111, 128, 147, 161, 163
Ohio Arts Council 178
Ohio Bell Telephone Company 13, 177
Ohio Cooperative Extension Service 78
Ohio Department of Natural Resources 16
Ohio Department of Taxation 78
Ohio Department of Wildlife 11
Ohio Division of ASC 164
Ohio Federation of Soil and Water Conservation Districts 90
Ohio Governor 117
Ohio History 30, 183
Ohio Pail Company 132
Ohio Peace Officers Training Academy 168
Ohio Power Siting Board 95
Ohio River 90, 116, 127
Ohio State 146
Ohio State Department of Transportation 116
Ohl, C. J. 169
Ohl, Hazel 50
oil 98; pails 132; return lines 137; wells 12, 19
Oklahoma Agricultural and Machanical College 192
Oklahoma State 192
Old Agricultural Society 84, 91
Old Man Winter 10
Old Plank Road 130
Old State Road 134, 144
Olympics 151
Oneida, NY 48
onions 93
Opera House Block 180
Opportunity School 71
Oral History Project 23, 25, 71, 192
Orchard Hills Golf and Country Club 146
orchard/s 146, 151
organ 50
organizations 163
Orr, Cynthia 174
Orwell (OH) 27, 40, 138
Otego, NY 27
outdoor 145, 159

Outdoor Ministries 51
Owen, Adelaide 50
Owne, Ben 92
oxen 81, 92, 98, 113
oxen-drawn equipment 124
Ozborne, Alice 55

P

pack-horse 115
paddle/s 88
pageant 92
pail/s 98, 102, 132
Paine, Edward, Capt. 115, 175
Painesville (OH) 23, 30, 33, 116, 165, 180, 181, 192
Painesville & Youngstown Railroad 116
Painesville and Hudson Company 116
Painesville Telegraph 25, 31
Painesville-Ravenna Road 116
paint 138; pails 132
Paleontology 24
pallets 127, 139
Palmer, Betty 93
Palmer, Isaac, Dr. 25
pan/s 98, 100, 106, 107
pancake flour 109
paneling 139
panfish 146
papoose 25
parade/s 73, 101, 141, 145, 155, 158, 164
paraformaldehyde 102
parent 174
parent-teacher organization/s 65, 164
parish 73
Park (Ave.) 73, 149; Apartments 15
Park Auditorium 65
Park Hotel 126
park/s 12, 13, 16, 17, 18, 95, 134, 144, 146, 154, 181; Division of 147
parking 125
Parkinson, Bliss 148
Parkman (OH) 26, 27, 29, 63, 77, 80, 82, 115, 117, 136, 153, 166, 178, 181, 183, 184
Parkman Band 123
Parkman Congregational Church 42
Parkman Township 59, 79
Parkman, Lucy (Phelps) 27
Parkman, Robert B. 26, 27
Parkman, Samuel 26
Parochial School Systems 69
Parsons, Dorothy 150, 179
Parsons, W. C. 175
Parting Song, The 51
Paskevich and Associates, Anthony 18
Patch, Laban, Dr. 29
Patchin, David 30
Patchin, Emily (Nash) 27, 28
Patchin, Philansia 30
Patterson Center 78, 87, 90, 112
Patterson, Mabel 112
Patterson, N. C. 112
Patton, Betty 66
paved 116, 119
pavers 124
Pavilion 148, 154
paving 123
Paving Company 124
Pealer, Leanne 7
Pediatrics 172
pellet 102
Pennell, Melissa 154
Pennell, William 154
Pennsylvania 21, 23, 78, 90, 115
pension/s 35, 40
Percival, E. J. 181
Perry Hanna Nuclear Power Plant 94, 95
Petersen, Peter 170
Petite 192
petroleum 116
pharmacies 141, 181
Phelps, Alfred 26
Phelps, Lucy 27
Phelps, Oliver 25
Phelps, Samuel W. 165
Philathea Class 50
Phileo (Love) 50
Phillips, R. L. 185
Phillips, Robert L. 116
photographer 83, 180
photographs 141
Pickett, Marilyn 173
Pickett, Merribell 133
pickpockets 91
picnic 146; area/s 144, 146
picnicking 15
pictorial history 183
pie/s 83, 84, 87; baking 158
pigs 84, 88
pike, northern 146
Pilgrim Christian Church 137
Pilgrims 87
pill 104
Pilla, Anthony M., Bishop 72
Pioneer and General History of Geauga County 183
Pioneer Association 29
Pioneer Road 53
Pioneer School 60, 61
Pioneer School House 59

Pioneer Village 87
Pioneer Waterland 146
pioneers 20-37; 127
Piper, A. 108
Pittsburgh (PA) 23, 52, 120, 178
pizza 151
Plain Dealer 78
Plainfield, MA 22
Plank Road 130
plaque 182
plastic/s 102, 137, 139; bags 98; jugs 110; tubing 98
plasticizing 141
plat 165
Plavcan, Debbie 170
Pleasant Hill Golf Course 146
Pleasant Hill Home 165, 171
Pleistocene Period 24
Pleva, Larry 159
pliers 105
Plum Bottom Creek 12
plumber 55
plumbing 106, 137
pockets 91
poetry 178
police 166
politics 116
Pollock Woods 98, 106
Pollock, Andrea 95
Pollock, Ernest 62
pollute 142
pollution 78
Pomeroy, Frank S., Dr. 167
Pomeroy, Stephen 28
ponds 146
ponies, Welsh 41
pool 146, 159
Pool, Levi P. 29
Pope Home 175
Pope, Lewis L. 175
Popovic, Florence 50
population 184, 185
porch 129
Portage County (OH) 12, 20, 95, 116, 146
Post House Restaurant 136
post office 37, 130, 138, 161, 172, 175
post road 115
poster contest 172
postmaster 175
potatoes 87, 100
Potter, NY 29
Poutasse, Charles 55, 169
poverty 145
power 80, 95; lines 94; plant/s 94, 95, 137
Pratt, B. H. 29
predators 11, 85
preparatory school 70
Presbyterian church 42
preserves 95
Price, Mary 65
Prior, Bill 142
Probate and Juvenile Court 163
Probate Court 165
Probate records 179
problems 164
products 113, 128
Progress Literary Club 174
Progress-Research 172
propeller 132
prosecutor 185
Prots Food Center 143
Public Affairs 163
Public Health 169
Public Square 91, 108, 183
public transportation 116, 125
publisher 179
pulley 84, 104
pulpit exchange 40
pump 104
Pumpkin Festival 145
pumpkins 33, 93
Punderson Lake 12, 147; State Park 146, 147
Punderson, Lemuel 29, 128, 147
Purdy, Lisa 73
pylons 140

Q

Quaker Oats Company 109
Quality Care 171
quarry/ies 6, 12, 13, 24, 25, 127
Queen 158
quill 113; pens 50
quilt 172
quilting 59

R

rabbit 97; mold 110
raccoon/s 21, 97, 148
Raccoon County Music Festival 145
race 152
racetrack 91
raceway 155
RACONTEUR 192
Radcliffe, Mary 174
radio 138, 178
radwaste 137
raffia wreaths 60
rags 133

railroad/s 115, 116
railway 116; station 161
rain 149
ram 99
Ramisch, Marjorie 172, 174
ramp 43
Randall Block 175, 179
Randall Mall 111
Randles, Ralph 62
random sampling 184
rangers 17
Ranney, — 28
Ravenna (OH) 108
Ravenna Road 117, 124
Ravenwood Mental Health Center 164, 170
realtor/s 154
Reap Realty, Thomas 61
Rebekah Lodges 164
rebuilding 179
recipe 111
Reckart, Kay 169
Recorder 185
Recorder's office 165
recount 184
recreation 111, 144-161; park 154
Red Barn 160
Red Jacket 21, 23
Reda, Reno 12
Redford, Shannon 70
Reese, Captain 83
Reformation 78
regulation/s 77, 139
Reker, Michael 73
religion 40
Rennie, David 110
renovating 64
renovation 41, 43, 69, 147
repairs 160
reptile 11
Republican 29, 177
Republican-Record 177
research 179
reservoir/s 12, 15, 117, 146
resort 148
restaurant 129
Restland Cemetery 81
restoration 110
Resusa Annie 142
ret 84
retailers 128
reunions 145
reverse osmosis 100, 106
Revolution 33, 35, 37
Reynolds, Denise 24
Rhodes, Anson 112
Rhodes, Ella 112
Rhodes, James A. 117
Ricca, Barbara 93
Richards Maple Products 102, 103, 109, 110, 113
Richards, Almeda M. 34
Richards, Austin 34, 109
Richards, Clara Jean 112
Richards Family 110
Richards, Paul 107, 109, 112
Richards, Rena 109, 112
Richards, Sally (Chadwick) 34
Richards, Will 112
Richards, William S. 109
Richmond, Bill 55
Rickard, C. E. 136
Rickard, Lewis 136
Rickard, Mark 136
Rickard, Robin 136
Riddle, Albert Gallatin (A.G.) 12, 28, 178
Rider Cemetery 33
Rider, Benjamin 33
Rider, Hannah 33
Rider, Polly 34
Ridge Road United Church of Christ 50
Rider Cemetery 33
Ritchie, Edith 134
rivalries 177
river/s 12, 13, 23, 25, 26, 116, 117, 146
Riverside High School 192
Riverview Church 38
Riverview Memorial Park Cemetery 38
road 26
roast 87
Robinson, Clark 37
Robinson, David 37
Robinson, Judy 94
Robinson, Ryan 113
Rock Creek Road 155
Rockathon 70
rocky 148
Rocky Cellar 13
Rolling Green Golf Club 146, 158
Rome, NY 35
Romeo and Juliet 65
Ronyak, A. J. 124
Ronyak, Sherry 158
Roose Drug Store 7, 23, 27, 69, 125, 141
Roose, Richard "Rick" 7, 141
rope 104
Rossiter, Cliff 93, 112
Rotary International 164, 192
Rothenbuhler, Hans R. 139
Route 6 116, 124
Route 44 108, 121, 148

ute 86 116, 130
ute 87 14, 63, 116, 138, 140, 141
ute 88 117
ute 168 116, 117, 153, 155
ute 306 116, 137, 148, 174
ute 322 116, 124, 130, 148, 165
ute 422 116, 136, 137, 146, 159, 173, 174
ute 528 117, 134, 146, 138
ute 608 63, 116, 119, 123, 134, 138, 141, 146
ute 700 116
owley, Addison H. 31
owley, Celestia Sophia 31
owley, Corydon T. 31
owley, Dimas 25
owley, Elizabeth (Williams) 31
owley, Ellen (Carter) 31
owley, Elosia (Andrews) 31
owley, Erastus 31
owley, Esther 31
owley, Etta 31
owley, Fayette 31
owley, Harrison 85
owley, Maria (Ensign) 31
owley, Maud 31
owley, Myra 31
owley, Robert 31
owley, Sherman 31
owley, Sherwood 31
owley, Sophia 31
owley, Sophia (Taylor) 31
owley, Tracy D. 31
bber 128, 137, 139; tube 132
ug and Craft Show 152
nway 117
upert, Chester C., Rev. 46
uritan 164
ussell (OH) 12, 14, 21, 37, 38, 48, 60, 69, 83, 90, 166, 184
ussell Center 12
ussell Haueter Excavating 170
ussell Park 16
ussell, Dorothy 23
ussell, Eldon 16
ussell, Gideon 37

S

Sabo, Elly 57
Saikaly, Gus 37
Sajar Plastics 169
salt 88
salt rising bread 136
Samuel, Frank 89
Sand Hill 11
Sanger, Etta 185
sap 97, 98, 99, 100, 101, 102, 103, 104, 105, 106, 108
sassafras 102
saturation 97
Saunders, Esther 174
Saunders, Mary Virginia 70
saw 130
sawmill/s 59, 80, 127, 129, 130, 139
sawyer 130
Saydah, Cindy 60
Schager, Nancy 150
Schinagle, Iola 7
Schlabach Printers 53
Schofield, Frank 59
school/s 58-74, 141, 142, 149, 170, 172, 173, 179, 180, 184, 185, 192; school/s private 69
School Board Clerk 192
School District 61, 62, 173
school levy 60
School Population 185
School-in-the-Woods 63
schoolbell 60
schoolbus 60
schoolin' 59
Schuler, Leland 112
Scotch Pines 90
Scotland General Store 130
Scotland stop 148
screw machine 137
screw plasticizing 141
scythe 84
Sea World 146, 180
Sealy, Edith 132
Sealy, T. J. 132
secretary 192
sediment 78
seedlings 90
Seenarine, Moolchan Mark, Rev. 51
Sekerak, Deborah 50, 82, 173
seminary 69
senators 163
Senior Citizens 170
senior clubs 170
Senior Newsletter 170
separator 84
Septaquintcentennial 30
Service Auction 55
services 128, 163-175
Sesquicentennial 41
settlement 20-37, 115
seven-layer salad 87
sewer 37
Shagg 180

Shamu 180
Shangri La Ski Club 153
Shanower Library 36
Shanower, B. J. 22, 61, 74, 87, 158, 172
Shanower, Ralph 62
Sheauga Quilters Guild 172
sheaves 84
sheep 85
Shellito, Howard 132
Shellito, Walter 132
shelter 164
Sheltered Workshop 71
Sheptak, Julia/e 56, 164
sheriff 165, 185
Sherman, — 28
Sherman, Zula 166
Shelter Printing 23, 27, 69, 178
Shelter, Garland 7, 109, 141
shine 83
shingles 32
Shipman, Don 169
Shippey, Horace 137
shocks 85, 87
shoe/s 113, 135; shop 181
shopping 128
Shopsmith 88
Short, Elizabeth 192
Sidley Company, R. W. 6, 138
Sidley Road 47, 155
Sidley, James D. 67
Sidley, Robert C. 138
Sidley, Robert W. 138
Sidley, William 47
silage 87
silica 6, 12, 127, 138; mining 183
silo 102; filler 87
Silver Jubilee 56
Simmons, — 179
Simons, Menno 78
sing 155
Sisson Road 146
Sister Mary Aimee 172, 173
Six Nations 21
ski 151; lodge 74
skids 139
skiers 74
skiing 147, 153; accident 139; cross-country 147
skills 127
Skinner, Abraham 165
skunk 97
sled 97, 98; hill 147
Sleeth, Natalie 80
Small Cities Program 168
Smith, Benjamin 27
Smith, Dan 70
Smith, Douglas 27
Smith, H. K., Judge 126
Smith, Joel 70
Smith, L. M. 126
Smith, Mary T. 185
Smith, Mercy 27
Smith, Murray S. 179, 183, 185
Smith, Stuart S. 179
Smith, Wilson 149
Smiths 8
Smoke Stoppers 175
snack bar 159
snow 19, 100, 101, 151; belt 12, 13, 151; blower 15
snowmobile 147
Snyder Road 32, 159, 173, 174
Sober, Edgar 28
soccer 146
Social Security 40
softball 146, 158
softening 142
soil 78
Soil and Water conservation District 7, 78
Solon, OH 110
Solon Branch Library 192
Solon Cleaners 143
somersault 44
Songs from the Hills 51
Sons of Temperance 164
Sound Effects 143
Sound of Music 65
South Hambden 34
South Main Street 138, 139
South Newbury 108, 121, 148
South Newbury Chapel 46
South Russell 69, 173
South Russell Village 163, 166, 187
South Street 149, 164, 183
Southhampton, MA 25
Sowkeys, Frank, Dr. 151
Spain 21
Specific Learning Disabilities 60
Speck, Nancy 63
spelldown 59
Sperry Lane 144
Sperry, Dorothea 112
Sperry, J. E. 129
Sperry, Kenneth 112
Sperry, Mark 17
spices 89
spiles 98, 102, 104
Spinners 64
spinning 133
spire 56

splitter 99
spontaneous combustion 181
Sports Haven 158
spouts 98, 102, 105
spring 99
Spurlock, Elsie 170
Spurlock, Mark 170
square 179; dancing 59
squash 93
squaw 25
squirrel/s 90, 105
St. Anselm School 72
St. Anselm's Church 72
St. Denis (golf) 146
St. Helen's Catholic Church 49, 71, 73; School 73
St. Helen's Unicycle Drill Team 49, 73
St. Luke's Day 56
St. Luke's Episcopal Church 56
St. Mark's Episcopal Church 57
St. Mary's 60; Church School 73
St. Patrick's Cemetery 47; Church; Day 73
stables 128, 149
Stafford, G. W. 129
stagecoach 35
stain 142
stainless tubing 137
stalks 84
Stamford, CT 137
Stanbery, G. W. 172
stand 91
Standard Oil Company (Ohio) 42, 45
Stanton, Hal 28
Stanton, Luman 28
Starr Quality Produce 93
Starr, Donald 93
Starr, Richard 62
State Library of Ohio 164
State Park, Punderson 146, 147
station/s 121, 122, 178
steam 97, 108; engine 84, 155
Stebbins, Judy 31
Steel 137; pails 132
steeple 44
stenciling 59
Steuben, NY 24
Stevens, Hepzibah 35
Stevens, Reuel 35
Stevens, Roswell 35
stewardship 179, 182
Stewart, Jan 93
Stigwandish, Camp 146
stilts 74
Stinson, Dorothy 174
Stith, Bari 169
stock 143
Stock Engineering Company 137
Stock Equipment Company 137
Stock, Arthur J. 137
Stocking, D. W. 126
stone ledge 136; mason 25, 117; quarries 127
Stone, Kelly 111
Stone, Nathaniel 30, 165
Stone, Vene, Judge 29
stone-arched bridge 117
storage tank 97, 103
store/s 127, 128, 130, 131, 134, 135, 161, 173, 175, 181
storefront 173
strainer 107
straining 97
Strate, Rowena Belle 24
straw 84, 85
strawberries 93
streams 12, 19, 115, 127
street light 123
Street Walking Through the Decades 170
Street, Josie 173
Street, Titus 22
streetcar 91
streets 123
stress 145
Strong, Willard, Rev. 28
Strum, William P. 24
Sturm, Inez (Chamberlen) 24
Sudyk, Billye 43
Suffield, CT 25
Suffolk sheep 85
sugar 89, 98, 110; bush 107, 108; cake 111; camp 100; candy 110; house 98, 100, 102, 103, 104, 112; making 97
sugarcake 110
sugared 100
sugaring off 106
suit 133
Sullivan, Margaruite 67
Summer Session 74
Summit County (OH) 12, 15
sunglasses 141
superintendent 59
surveying 115
SWCD 78
Sweetbriar Lane 14
Swift, John 124
swimming 147, 153, 159
Swine Creek Park 16, 17
Swiss Chese 139; Festival 141, 145, 156
Switzerland, Berne 139
Swonger, James 62

syrup 100, 102, 104, 106, 107, 108, 110, 112
Syrup Producers' 90

T

tableware 141
Taborville 151
taffy 59
Talarcek, Andrew 62
Talarcek, Ann 62
Talarcek, Elsie 62
Talarcek, Josephine 62
Talbot, John 42
Talcott, Ellen 92
Talcott, Fred 92
Talley, Terry 66
Tanglewood Country Club 146
Tanglewood Mall 128
tank/s 97, 100, 104; canning 107; collecting 104; gathering 103
Tannehill, Joseph K. 137
tapped 100
tapping/s 98, 102
taps 104
tax 60
taxi 125
Taylor, Horace 31
Taylor, Howard 112
Taylor, Lester, Judge 37, 98, 145
Taylor, Lucretia 131
Taylor, Sophia 31
teacher/s 66
Teague Shopping Center 143
teamster/s 84, 92
technical services 172
Teed, Julian Czar 52
Teeter 192
telephone 164, 177
television 178
Temperance Hotel 180
temperature 82, 88
Temple, Art 170
Tempura dinner 55
tennis 147; courts 144, 159
tent 147
terrain 115
tests 59
tether ball 161
Thanksgiving Day 32
Thayer, Gertrude 172
theater/s 138, 170
thermoset 141
Thomas, Lloyd 155
Thompson (OH) 6, 12, 24, 25, 47, 60, 67, 116, 117, 133, 138, 155, 166, 171, 181, 184
Thompson Avenue 63
Thompson Drag Raceway 155
Thompson High School 67
Thompson House 134
Thompson Ledges Park Museum 181
Thompson Ledges Township Park 13
Thompson, Library Station 172
Thompson Silica Company 6, 138
Thompson United Methodist Church 46
Thompson, Eugenia/e 50, 134
Thompson, Henry 134
Thompson, Isaac 23, 134
Thompson, Isabel 23
Thompson, James 23
Thompson, Jane 23
Thompson, Matthew 25
Thompson, Ward 131
Thrasher House 56
Thrasher, — 28
Thrasher, Art 92
Thrasher, James Quentin 101
Threshermen's Convention 84
threshing 83
Thrift Shop 49
timber 127
Times-Leader 7, 78, 177, 178, 184
Timmons, Clare 112
Timmons, Dick 112
Timmons, George 112
Timmons, Ruth 112
tin 98, 110
Tincher, Don 159
Titus, Karen 65
tobaccos 29
toboggan hill 147
Todd, James C. 164, 185
Toledo (OH) 132
Tolles, Abbey 173
tomahawk 98
tomatoes 93
Tompkins, Keith 56
Tonawandas 21
Toogood, Maria 172
tools 105
tornado/es 13, 14
tours 17
tower/s 94, 95
town plat 165
Town, Ava 50
Town, Lucie 50
township park/s 13, 141, 146
townships 116, 154, 163, 164, 182
toxic 142
track 91, 149

traction 116, 121
tractor/s 85, 97, 99, 124
trailer 147, 161
trains 120, 128
transportation 62, 114-125, 128, 184
Trask, Noma A. 34
travel 111
Travel Time 184
treasurer 163, 165, 185
tree/s 11, 63, 97, 98, 99, 100, 102, 104, 136, 182; packet 90; planting 65, 66
trough 97
trout 146
Troy (OH) 12, 16, 22, 28, 28, 30, 33, 62, 77, 113, 166, 175, 184
Troy Northeast District 53
Troyer, John J. 53
Troyer, Nevin 53
Troyer, Noah B. 53
truck/s 107, 124, 161
Trumbull County (OH) 20, 21, 61, 115, 116, 138
Trumbull County Boy Scout Council 153
trustee/s 93, 116, 154, 163, 171, 172, 173
Trybus, Mona 172, 173
tubing 105, 137, 140
Tucek Science Center, Frank M. 66
tuition 62
turntable 124
twister 14

U

UCC (United Church of Christ) 40
Ucchino, Michael 142
Udall-Shellito Company 132
Ule, Andy 158
Umberfield Coffee House 22
Umberfield Log Cabin 22
Umberfield Tavern 180
Umberfield, Lydia 22
Umberfield, Thomas 22
undertaker 132
undertaking 131
unicycle 49, 73
Union Block 175
Union Chapel 46
United Protestant Church 51
United States 145, 151
United Way 64
Universalists 45
Unusual (OH) 37
utilities 77

V

Vaccariello, Bud 41
vacuum 100, 104
valves 106
Van Allen, Robert 150
Van Orsdale, Otto 131
Varga, Carol 173
Vaughn, Gladys 155
vegetable/s 80, 87; seedlings 93
Veit, Hans 163
veneer 130
Vermont 29, 30, 37, 109, 110
Veterans of Foreign Wars (V.F.W.) 164
Vicki 17
Vietnamese 40
village/s 116, 122, 163, 164 (see also individual names)
Village Booksellers 143
visually handicapped 146, 150
Vocational Wing 66
Vokoun, Susan 64
volunteer/s 17, 47, 87, 166, 167, 171, 175, 179
Volunteer Bureau 164
Volunteer Fire Department 166
Volunteer Recognition Dinner 164

W

wagon/s 81, 85, 97, 108, 129
Wahl, Jack 158
Wahl, John 158
Wahl, Richard 158
wallets 91
walleye 146
war 40, 138
War of 1812 32
Ward, Ed 85
Ward, Judy (Hunt) 85
Warfield, Chuck 32
Warne, Earle 169
Warne, Wade 27
Warner, — Dr. 167
Warner, Zophar 33
Warren (OH) 23, 30, 33, 108, 148
Warren (NH) 29
Warren, Deborah 154
Warren, Gary 154
Warren, Jim 117, 133, 154
Warren, Violet 7, 23, 28, 43, 50, 84, 133, 183
Warrensville Branch Library 192
washers 137
Washington Post Center 143
Washington Street 137, 143, 173, 174
Washington, George 182
water 11, 26, 78, 80, 84, 88, 89, 100, 104, 105,
106, 115, 142; amusement 146; monkey 84; processing industry 142; resources 153; skiing 153; sports 153; springs 128; trough 160
Water Street 164
Waterloo 106
Waterplant 142
waterslides 146
waterwheels 25
WBKC AM 178
WCDN AM 178
weather 12, 115, 182
Weaver, Pete M. 53
Weaver, Sam 78
weavers 64
weaving 133
Webb, Dora Jean 62
Webb, Mildred 62
Weber, Robert F. 168
wedge 99
Weekly Mail 178
weights 43
Welch, Dana, Rev. 45
Welchman, Nellie 132
Welchman, S. S. 132
welfare 40
Wellman, Andrew 62
Wellman Ann 62
Wellman, Ellis 84
Wellman Jean 62
Wellman, Mary 62
wellness 175
Wells, J. C. 84, 91
Wells, Jefferson, Rev. 51
Wells, Kim, Rev. 51
Wells, Steve 125
Welsh, Adrian 139
Welsh, Betsey 30
Welsh, Jacob 30
Welshfield (OH) 30, 116; Inn 129
Werft, Sandra 172
Wesleyan Methodist 30, 49
West Center Street 180
West Claridon 44
West Geauga 185; Board of Education 174; High School 69; School District 69, 185
West Park Street 180
West, David, Rev. 44
Western Reserve 20, 115, 116; Historical Society 97; Spinners and Weavers Guild 64; Telephone Company 177
wetlands 95
Weygant, A. C. 181
whale 180
wheat weaving 59
Wheeler, Anna 67
Wheeler, Robert A. 30, 183
Wheeling (WV) 178
Wheeling & Lake Erie Railroad 116
When the Spirit Says, "Sing" 51
whetstone 84
Whig/s party 177, 178
Whipkey, Marilyn 15, 19, 37, 56, 74, 168, 169
Whipple, Paul, Rev. 49
whiskey 25
White Brothers 142; Plaza 119; Super Market 138;
White Motor Company 70
White, Basil 138
White, Chuck 94
White, George 61, 142
White, Graydon 138
White, Graydon, Sr. 138
White, Lawrence 138
White, Lloyd 138
White, Ralph 138
White, Thomas L. 112
White, Virgil 138
White, Walter 70
White, Will 138
Whitewood Board 39
Whitewood, Handsome 42
Whitewood tree 42
Whitlam Woods 16
Whitney, Charlene 30
Wiggins, Sylvia 7, 23, 25, 37, 91, 104, 130, 148
wilderness 115
wildlife 11, 78
William Gilbert Hotel 181
Williams Farm 90
Williams, Elizabeth 31
Williams, Esther 65
Williams, Evelyn 173
Williams, Jim 179
Williams, Laurita 90
Williams, Michael 24
Williams, Robert 90
Williams, Roy, Rev. 45
Williams, Sieglinde 172, 174
Williams, Thomas 83
Wilmot, Kenneth 62
Wilson Mills Road 56
Wilson, Helen 172
Wilson, Maude 67
Wimbledon Ballroom 159
Winchell, Martha 24
windrow 85
Windsor (OH) 116
wine and cheese festival 72
winter 82, 89, 152
winterizing 168
Wise, Camp 146
witnesses 95
Wolfe, Emma Ella 27
Womanless Wedding 150
Women's Guild 49
Womensafe 164
Wood, Arthur 183
wood-church 97
Woodbury House 185
Woodbury B. B. 185
Woodhill, NY 24
Woodin Road Park 16
wood/s 94, 98, 99
wool 133
Wooster (OH) 23
workshop 142
World War I 135, 174, 181
World War II 40, 101, 136, 138, 192
World's Columbian Exposition 104
World's Fair 109
WPHR 108 178
Wright, Benjamin 33
Wright, Eliza Clapp 134
writing 60

Y

Yankee/s 40, 78, 82, 107, 136, 143
yardstick 97
Yesteryear in the Park 158
Yesteryear Queen 158
YMCA 146
Yoder, Belva 50
Yoder, Clara 87
Yoder, Crist A. 53
yoke 98
Young Authors 178
Young Country 178
Young, Don 139
Young, Merribell (Pickett) 133
Youngstown Macaroni Company (OH) 135

Z

Zakany, George 141, 169
Zavodny, Jill 168
Zebehazy, Alexander J. 182
Zebehazy, Margaret McLean 182
Zeller, Lenn, Rev. 42

Jeannette Grosvenor is a native Geaugan and the sixth generation of her family to live in the home built in 1833 in Claridon Township. She was nicknamed "Teeter" before one year old, a derivation of being called "Petite" by an uncle who had been in France during World War I.

A graduate of Burton High School (now Berkshire), she was a Pharmacist's Mate 3/c during World War II, and graduated from Oklahoma Agricultural and Mechanical College (now Oklahoma State) with a degree in Bacteriology. She has taught school in Claridon, Chardon, and Hambden, and served as School Board Clerk and school secretary. She has worked as an accountant and been self-employed as a carpenter and cabinet maker.

In retirement, her energy is devoted to collecting Geauga's history and genealogy. She is the author of *Descendants of Nathan & Laura (Fuller) Grosvenor*; *The ABC's of The First Congregational Church of Claridon, Ohio*; co-author of *A Monumental Work; Inscriptions & Interments in Geauga County, Ohio, Through 1983*; editor of *RACONTEUR* (newsletter of the Geauga County Genealogical Society); and co-editor of *Geaugaspeak*, quarterly of the Oral History Project of Kent State University, Geauga Campus.

James J. Anderson was born and raised in Painesville, Ohio. He is a graduate of Painesville Riverside High School. He earned his Bachelor of Science Degree in Mathematics from Mount Union College in Alliance, Ohio, and his Master of Science Degree in Library Science from Case Western Reserve University, Cleveland, Ohio.

Jim has been at Geauga County Public Library since 1982, and manager of the Chardon Library since 1984. Prior to that he had worked at the Solon and Warrensville Branches of Cuyahoga County Public Library, and the Burton Public Library.

He married Elizabeth (Short) Anderson in 1976. Jim and Betsy have three children, Christopher John, Adam James, and Sarah Elizabeth. Jim moved to Geauga County in 1972, and with his family now lives in Burton.

The Andersons are proprietors of Cottage Pottery in Burton and are members of Chardon United Methodist church. They are also actively involved in Marriage Encounter United Methodist. Jim is a member of Chardon Rotary Club.